knitted critters

for kids to wear

knitted critters

for kids to wear

MORE THAN 40 ANIMAL-THEMED ACCESSORIES

Jean Adel

POTTER CRAFT

NEW YORK

I dedicate this book to my husband, Adel, the wind beneath my wings; to my late and dear mother Grace, who taught me the beauty and joy of creativity; to my father, Edward, and his wife, Maxine, for their steadfast support and encouragement; and to my dear brother, Jeff, for supplying the endless parade of creatures that became the inspiration for these projects. You are all so dear to my heart.

Copyright © 2008 by Jean Adel

Photographs copyright © 2008 by Potter Craft
Illustrations copyright © 2006 by Potter Craft

All illustrations were originally published in Nature Babies by
Tara Jon Manning (Potter Craft, 2006).

Library of Congress Cataloging-in-Publication Data

Adel, Jean.
   Knitted critters for kids to wear : more than 40 animal-themed accessories / Jean Adel.
      p. cm.
   Includes index.
   ISBN 978-0-307-39466-8
   1. Knitting—Patterns. 2. Children's clothing. 3. Animals in art. I. Title.
   TT825.A294 2008
   746.43'2041--dc22   2007029553

ISBN 978-0-307-39466-8

Printed in China

Photography by Dan Howell
Prop Styling by Leslie Siegel
Fashion Styling by Kristen Petliski
Illustrations by Gayle Isabelle Ford
Design by La Tricia Watford

10 9 8 7 6 5 4 3

First Edition

Photo on page 2: Quacker the Duck, page 47, with Calypso the Whale, page 48. Photos on page 5: Jeremiah the Frog scarf and mittens, page 15; Wanda the Fish, page 76; and Wag the Dog, page 74. Photos on Page 7: Sydney the Koala Bear, page 19; Woody the Beaver, page 16; Boing the Bunny, page 20; and Minky the Cat, page 21.

contents

introduction

This book is dedicated to the creative spirit in all of us. It has been designed to meet the needs of all knitters—from absolute beginners to those who are a little more accomplished. It will give you the tools to explore the endless possibilities of mixing and matching, adding embellishments, and experimenting with color in a creative and imaginative way to fashion a truly unique collection of accessories for kids.

Each of the twenty patterns here is a combination of hats, mix-and-match scarves, and mittens. None of the projects requires more than basic knitting skills, and all have been selected to deliver the greatest impact with the least amount of time commitment.

I developed an interest in knitting when I was a young girl, and never lost my love for it. I am so passionate about knitting in all of its facets that I pursued it as a livelihood, becoming a senior editor at both *Vogue Knitting* and *Family Circle Easy Knitting* magazines, and even designed my own line of children's knitwear, which is carried by high-end retailers such as Barneys. Over the years, I've learned what every knitter wants: simple, fun projects that work up in no time and are as enjoyable to make as they are to give and wear.

With our hectic lives and limited leisure time, the need for quick, simple, stand-out projects is great. I have often heard people say they don't have time to knit. You'd be surprised

how much time you actually have. A moment stolen here and there can add up to a hat, scarf, and mittens in no time. Think of the idle time you spend waiting in line at the bank, at the doctor or dentist, commuting to work, taking lunch breaks at the office, and watching TV at the end of the day. Start your holiday knitting on the bus; finish the mittens on your lunch hour; and slip in a few rows on that scarf while watching your favorite sitcom. It's just that simple. Transform those little windows of opportunity into precious presents for your loved ones and friends. These easy-to-make patterns will make it even easier.

Consider this book a collection of templates and starting points to let your imagination soar. Experiment with fluffy faux fur, wool–mohair blends, smooth wool, and luxurious angora yarn. A variety of textures and colors produces entirely different looks with every project. This book is about taking a basic pattern and making it your own—choosing your own colors, yarns, textures, and finishing details. It's those little touches here and there—like a pom-pom or embroidered nose, button or wiggle eyes, or embroidered mouth—that will set your knit critters apart from the rest.

So get knitting. Let your creative spirit take over, experiment, and have fun.

Please stay in touch and come visit us at www.JeanAdel.com

THE BASICS AND MATERIALS

A child's hat, scarf, and mitten set is a rewarding project to make. Small, simple projects require little investment of time and materials and are ideal for experimenting with new yarns (Sydney the Koala Bear, page 19), new colors (Wanda the Fish, page 76), new techniques (Ringo the Dog, page 75), or new embellishments (Whinny the Horse, page 51). But before you begin, make sure you review the information in this chapter.

BASIC TOOLS

You will want to acquire a few basic and inexpensive tools before you start knitting. Keep them handy inside a zippered pouch in your knitting bag along with your project, so you'll have everything you need to knit on all of your travels.

- Small, sharp scissors
- Yarn needle (Chibi needles with bent tips are best—they enable you to slip the tip of the needle under stitches with ease)
- Retractable tape measure
- Stitch markers
- Stitch holders
- Point protectors
- Row counter
- Needle gauge ruler (for measuring stitches and rows in a gauge swatch or your project)
- Crochet hook (medium-size)
- Knitting needles (straight, double-pointed, and circular)
- Sticky notes (to keep track of where you are in a pattern or chart)
- Pen (to make notes)

SIZING

All the hats, scarves, and mittens in this book are written in three sizes, Small (3 years), Medium (4–5 years), and Large (6–7 years). For mittens, the smallest size is written as a thumbless version. Thumbless mittens are easy to slip on and off small hands and keep little fingers warm and toasty. The other two pattern sizes—Medium and Large—have a thumb. For accurate sizing, take your child's hand measurements, both the circumference (at the widest point) and the hand length. For hat sizing, measure just above the ears (at the widest point) to obtain the circumference. A general note on sizing: When in doubt, go up a size.

GAUGE

A gauge swatch takes only a few minutes to make and will provide you with all the information you need to knit a project that will fit the way you want.

Gauge is the number of stitches and rows per inch and determines the size of the project you are making. Make a test gauge swatch at least 4" (10cm) square, using the yarn and needle size called for in the pattern. You may need to adjust your needle size in order to obtain the gauge required. Then, measure your swatch carefully, including fractions of stitches. If the number of stitches and rows does not match the pattern's gauge, then you must change your needle size. To get fewer stitches to the inch, use a larger needle; to get more stitches to the inch, use a smaller needle size.

YARN SELECTION

There is an overwhelming variety of yarns on the market today and each produces an entirely different look. Fiber content includes both natural and synthetic, such as fluffy faux furs, smooth wools, fluffy angora, and fuzzy mohair–wool blends. Just be sure to purchase enough to complete your project, and note the shade and dye lot number on the ball band to ensure that each skein/ball is exactly the same color. To reproduce the projects as you see them photographed, use the yarns listed in the materials section of the patterns, which are readily available in knitting shops across the country. The Resources on page 94 provide contact information to help you locate retailers in your area.

YARN SUBSTITUTION

If you wish to substitute yarns, you will need to swatch until you achieve the pattern gauge. (For more information about gauge, see the section at left.) Once this has been accomplished, figure out how much substitute yarn you will need. First, determine the total length of the original yarn in the pattern by multiplying the number of skeins/balls listed by the yards/meters per ball/skein. Divide this figure by the new yards/meters per ball of your substitute yarn (listed on the ball band) and round up to the next whole number. This will give you the number of balls/skeins you need to purchase.

WASHING INSTRUCTIONS

Be sure to read the ball band and follow the manufacturer's suggested method of laundering. If you're in doubt about whether to machine wash, wash your project by hand, using warm water and a mild detergent. Be careful not to agitate or the friction may produce a felted effect. Roll your project in a towel, press the water out, gently pat into shape, and allow to air dry.

READING CHARTS

Unlike patterns that are written out in rows, charts provide graphic representations of your knitting and are very easy to use. Each square represents a stitch, and each horizontal row a new row of stitches. Charts are usually read from bottom to top. The row numbers typically start at the bottom right-hand corner, so you follow a chart by reading from right to left for right-side rows. Wrong-side rows are read from left to right. Always follow the row numbers on the chart. The chart for Wag the Dog (page 84) begins on a wrong-side row, so the first row is read left to right. Charts indicate how the work will look on the right side. The color key explains where to use the different colors of yarns.

COLORWORK KNITTING

intarsia • is a method that uses separate lengths or balls of yarn for adding isolated areas of color, either large or small. The yarn is not carried across the back. When changing colors, pick up the new strand and wrap it around the strand of the main color before you begin knitting with it to prevent holes from forming in your work. For the projects featured in this book, you need only wind small balls of yarn. Since the projects are little, they do not require much yarn.

stranded knitting • allows you to knit small, allover color patterns by alternating colors and carrying the unused strand on the wrong side of the work. When stranding, it is very important to keep your tension loose to avoid pulling and distorting the knitted fabric.

FINE FINISHES

safety • do not use small buttons or safety eyes on hats, mittens, or scarves intended for use by babies or children under three years old, as they may cause a choking hazard if swallowed. For children under three, substitute duplicate stitch in the place of buttons and wiggle, animal, or frog eyes.

tassels • add a simple decorative finishing touch to your projects and are very simple to make. You start by wrapping the yarn around a piece of 3" (7.5cm) heavy cardboard about thirty-five times. Tie the strands together at one edge of the cardboard with a 12" (30.5cm) length of yarn. Cut the strands at the opposite edge. Tie another strand of yarn around the tassel, about ½" (1.5cm) below the top tie for the tassel neck. Thread the ends of the neck tie through the tassel. Trim the ends of the tassel evenly. Thread the ends of the top tie through the top corner of the hat, scarf, or mitten cuff and knot on the wrong side to secure.

01 | Beginner

Jeremiah the Frog

Froggy went a' ccurtin' in his (or her) charming hat, scarf, and mitten set. Knit on circular and double-pointed needles and embellished with simple embroidery and buttons or purchased frog eyes, this set is perfect for your little tadpole.

Instructions on page 24.

Woody the Beaver

This busy little beaver's ears are knit in the round and pleated as they're sewn to the hat—
no tricky knitting! Purchased eyes and a pom-pom nose make finishing quick and easy.

Instructions on page 27.

Henry the Hippo

Hip, hippo, hooray! Get the look with French knot nostrils and adorable ears—knit them in the round and sew them on upside-down.

Instructions on page 31.

Otto the Pig

Separate inner and outer ears add dimension to this hat knit in the round on circular and double-pointed needles.
Wiggle eyes and a button nose make for a quick, cute finish. Everyone who sees it will squeal with delight!

Instructions on page 32.

Sydney the Koala Bear

G'day mate! A felt nose and store-bought eyes complete this koala's sweet face. The small amount of angora used in this hat and mitten set is a luxurious treat that won't break the bank.

Instructions on page 34.

Boing the Bunny

Keep your favorite bunny warm as he or she hippity-hops around all winter. This bunny's face is embroidered, and her floppy ears are knit in the round with slipped stitches at the sides to make them lie flat.

Instructions on page 37.

Minky the Cat

Contrasting colors and textures combine to make this hat the cat's meow. The seed stitch pattern is as easy as knit 1, purl 1, and the soft merino yarn is comfortable for even the most sensitive kids.

Instructions on page 40.

Blizzard the Polar Bear

All aboard the Polar Bear Express! The stuffed ears on the top of this hat really stand out—use store-bought filling if you already have it or scraps of matching yarn. Pom-pom and button embellishments turn hats into bears. Ferocious or friendly? Your choice!

Instructions on page 42.

Cheddar the Mouse

Merino yarn makes this mouse extra snuggly. The outer ears are knit in the round, and the inner ears are knit flat separately and sewn on. Thread strands of yarn behind his pom-pom nose for easy whiskers.

Instructions on page 44.

Jeremiah the Frog

(shown on page 15)

SIZES

3 years (4–5 years, 6–7 years)

FINISHED MEASUREMENTS

scarf: 5 x 21 (25, 29)" (12.5 x 53.5 [63.5, 74]cm)
hat circumference: 16 (18, 20)" (40.5 [45.5, 51]cm)
mitten length: 5½ (7, 9½)" (14 [18, 24]cm)
circumference: 5½ (6½, 8)" (14 [16.5, 20.5]cm)

MATERIALS

- 2 skeins Brown Sheep Lamb's Pride Worsted, 85% wool, 15% mohair (4 oz [113.5g], 190 yd [173.5m]), #M120 Limeade **4 medium**
- Size 7 (4.5mm) 16" (40cm) circular needle
- Size 7 (4.5mm) double-pointed needles, set of 5
- Size 5 (3.75mm) double-pointed needles, set of 5
- Stitch markers
- Stitch holder (for Medium and Large mittens only)
- Yarn needle
- 4 black buttons, ½" (13mm) in diameter
- 2 black buttons or 2 frog eyes, ¾" (19mm) in diameter
- Small amount of black worsted-weight yarn

GAUGE

18 stitches and 25 rows = 4" (10cm) in stockinette stitch worked with a circular needle.

NOTE

The instructions are written for the smallest size, with changes for larger sizes in parentheses. For ease in working, circle all numbers pertaining to your size.

HAT

Using the circular needle, cast on 72 (80, 88) stitches. Join, being careful not to twist stitches. Place a marker for the beginning of the round. Work in stockinette stitch (knit every round) until the piece measures 4½ (5, 5½)" (11.5 [12.5, 14]cm) from the beginning.

shape crown

NOTE: Change to the larger double-pointed needles when the number of stitches has been sufficiently decreased.

Round 1: *K6, k2tog; repeat from * around—63 (70, 77) stitches.

Round 2: Knit.

Round 3: *K5, k2tog; repeat from * around—54 (60, 66) stitches.

Round 4: Knit.

Round 5: *K4, k2tog; repeat from * around—45 (50, 55) stitches.

Round 6: Knit.

Round 7: *K3, k2tog; repeat from * around—36 (40, 44) stitches.

Round 8: Knit.

Round 9: *K2, k2tog; repeat from * around—27 (30, 33) stitches.

Round 10: Knit.

Round 11: *K1, k2tog; repeat from * around—18 (20, 22) stitches.

Round 12: Knit.

Round 13: K2tog around—9 (10, 11) stitches.

Cut the yarn, leaving a long end. Use the yarn needle to thread the end through the remaining stitches. Draw together tightly and fasten off.

EYE (make 2)

Using the larger double-pointed needles, cast on 20 stitches. Divide the stitches onto 4 needles—5 stitches per needle. Join, being careful not to twist stitches. Place a marker for the beginning of the round.

Rounds 1–4: Knit.

Round 5: On the first needle, k2tog, k to the end of the needle; on the second needle, k to the last 2 stitches, k2tog; on the third needle, k2tog, k to the end of needle; on the fourth needle, k to the last 2 stitches, k2tog—4 stitches remain on each needle.

Rounds 6–7: Repeat round 5 twice—2 stitches remain on each needle. Slip stitches from the first and second needles onto the first needle; slip stitches from the third and fourth needles onto the third needle. Cut the yarn, leaving a long end. Hold the first and third needles parallel to each other and use the yarn end to graft the stitches together.

FINISHING

Sew a large button to one side of each Eye or attach a frog eye. Stuff the Eye with about 60" (152.5cm) of matching yarn. Sew Eyes to the top of the Hat. With black yarn, embroider a back-stitch mouth and nose on the Hat. Weave in ends.

SCARF

Using the circular needle, cast on 23 stitches. Work back and forth on cir-cular needle (as if working on straight needles).

Rows 1–6: Knit.

Row 7 (right side): Knit.

Row 8 (wrong side): K5, p to last 5 stitches, k5.

Repeat rows 7–8 until the piece mea-sures 20 (24, 28)" (51 [61, 71]cm) from the beginning.

Repeat rows 1–6 once.

Bind off.

FINISHING

Weave in ends.

MITTENS (make 2)
FOR SIZE SMALL ONLY

Using the smaller double-pointed needles, cast on 24 stitches. Divide the stitches evenly onto 4 needles, 6 stitches per needle. Join, being care-ful not to twist the stitches. Place a marker for the beginning of the round.

wrist ribbing

Work in k1, p1 rib for 1½" (3.8cm).

hand

Change to the larger double-pointed needles and work in stockinette stitch until the piece measures 4½" (11.5cm) from the beginning.

shape top

Round 1: *K2, k2tog; repeat from * around—18 stitches.

Round 2: Knit.

Round 3: *K1, k2tog; repeat from * around—12 stitches.

Round 4: Knit.

Round 5: *K2tog; repeat from * around—6 stitches.

Round 6: Knit.

Round 7: *K2tog; repeat from * around—3 stitches.

Cut the yarn, leaving a long end. Use the yarn needle to thread the end through the remaining stitches. Draw together tightly and fasten off.

FOR SIZES MEDIUM (LARGE)

Using the smaller double-pointed needles, cast on 30 (36) stitches. Divide the stitches onto 4 needles. Join, being careful not to twist the stitches. Place a marker for the beginning of the round.

wrist ribbing

Work in k1, p1 rib for 2 (3)" (5 [7.5]cm).

lower hand

Change to larger double-pointed needles.

Rounds 1–3 (5): Knit.

shape thumb gusset

Round 1: K14 (17), place a marker, increase in each of the next 2 stitches, place a marker, k to the end of the round—32 (38) stitches.

Round 2: Knit.

Round 3: K to marker, slip marker, increase in the next stitch, k to 1 stitch before the next marker, increase in the next stitch, slip marker, k to the end of round—34 (40) stitches.

Round 4: Knit.

Rounds 5–6 (8): Repeat the last 2 rounds 1 (2) time(s)—36 (44) stitches, with 8 (10) stitches between markers. Slip the stitches between the markers to a holder for the thumb.

Round 7 (9): Knit, casting on 2 stitches over the stitches on the holder—30 (36) stitches.

upper hand

Knit in rounds until the piece measures 2 (3)" (5 [7.5]cm) above the thumb gusset.

shape top

Round 1: *K4, k2tog; repeat from * around—25 (30) stitches.

Rounds 2, 4, 6, and 8: Knit.

Round 3: *K3, k2tog; repeat from * around—20 (24) stitches.

Round 5: *K2, k2tog; repeat from * around—15 (18) stitches.

Round 7: *K1, k2tog; repeat from * around—10 (12) stitches.

Round 9: *K2tog; repeat from * around—5 (6) stitches.

Cut the yarn, leaving a long end. Use the yarn needle to thread the end through the remaining stitches. Draw together tightly and fasten off.

thumb

Slip thumb stitches from the holder back to 1 larger double-pointed needle. Join yarn and cast on 4 stitches—12 (14) stitches. Work back and forth on 2 double-pointed needles in stockinette stitch (knit on right side, purl on wrong side) until the thumb measures 1½ (2)" (3.8 [5]cm) from the last row of the thumb gusset, ending with a wrong-side row.

Next row: K2tog across—6 (7) stitches.

Cut the yarn, leaving a long end. Use the yarn needle to thread the end through the remaining stitches. Draw together tightly and fasten off.

FINISHING

Sew the thumb seam on the Medium and Large Mittens.

Sew 2 smaller buttons to one side of each Mitten for the eyes. With black yarn, embroider a backstitch mouth and nose under the button eyes on each Mitten.

Weave in ends.

Woody the Beaver

(shown on page 16)

SIZES

3 years (4–5 years, 6–7 years)

FINISHED MEASUREMENTS

scarf: 5 x 21 (25, 29)" (12.5 x 53.5 [63.5, 74]cm)

hat circumference: 16 (18, 20)" (40.5 [45.5, 51]cm)

mitten length: 5½ (7, 9½)" (14 [18, 24]cm)

circumference: 5½ (6½, 8)" (14 [16.5, 20.5]cm)

MATERIALS

- 2 skeins Brown Sheep Lamb's Pride Worsted, 85% wool, 15% mohair (4 oz [113.5g], 190 yd [173.5m]), #M07 Sable **medium**
- Small amounts black and white worsted-weight yarn
- Size 7 (4.5mm) 16" (40cm) circular needle
- Size 7 (4.5mm) double-pointed needles, set of 5
- Size 5 (3.75mm) double-pointed needles, set of 5
- Stitch markers
- Stitch holder (for Medium and Large mittens only)
- 2 brown animal (crystal) eyes, ½" (13mm) in diameter
- Craft glue
- 5 brown pom-poms, 1" (25mm) in diameter
- Yarn needle

GAUGE

18 stitches and 25 rows = 4" (10cm) in stockinette stitch worked with a circular needle.

NOTE

The instructions are written for the smallest size, with changes for larger sizes in parentheses. For ease in working, circle all numbers pertaining to your size.

HAT

Using the circular needle, cast on 72 (80, 88) stitches. Join, being careful not to twist the stitches. Place a marker for the beginning of the round. Work in stockinette stitch (knit every round) until the piece measures 4½ (5, 5½)" (11.5 [12.5, 14]cm) from the beginning.

shape crown

NOTE: Change to the larger double-pointed needles when the number of stitches has been sufficiently decreased.

Round 1: *K6, k2tog; repeat from * around—63 (70, 77) stitches.

Round 2: Knit.

Round 3: *K5, k2tog; repeat from * around—54 (60, 66) stitches.

Round 4: Knit.

Round 5: *K4, k2tog; repeat from * around—45 (50, 55) stitches.

Round 6: Knit.

Round 7: *K3, k2tog; repeat from * around—36 (40, 44) stitches.

Round 8: Knit.

Woody the Beaver

(shown on page 16)

SIZES

3 years (4–5 years, 6–7 years)

FINISHED MEASUREMENTS

scarf: 5 x 21 (25, 29)" (12.5 x 53.5 [63.5, 74]cm)

hat circumference: 16 (18, 20)" (40.5 [45.5, 51]cm)

mitten length: 5½ (7, 9½)" (14 [18, 24]cm)

circumference: 5½ (6½, 8)" (14 [16.5, 20.5]cm)

MATERIALS

- 2 skeins Brown Sheep Lamb's Pride Worsted, 85% wool, 15% mohair (4 oz [113.5g], 190 yd [173.5m]), #M07 Sable **4 medium**
- Small amounts black and white worsted-weight yarn
- Size 7 (4.5mm) 16" (40cm) circular needle
- Size 7 (4.5mm) double-pointed needles, set of 5
- Size 5 (3.75mm) double-pointed needles, set of 5
- Stitch markers
- Stitch holder (for Medium and Large mittens only)
- 2 brown animal (crystal) eyes, ½" (13mm) in diameter
- Craft glue
- 5 brown pom-poms, 1" (25mm) in diameter
- Yarn needle

GAUGE

18 stitches and 25 rows = 4" (10cm) in stockinette stitch worked with a circular needle.

NOTE

The instructions are written for the smallest size, with changes for larger sizes in parentheses. For ease in working, circle all numbers pertaining to your size.

HAT

Using the circular needle, cast on 72 (80, 88) stitches. Join, being careful not to twist the stitches. Place a marker for the beginning of the round. Work in stockinette stitch (knit every round) until the piece measures 4½ (5, 5½)" (11.5 [12.5, 14]cm) from the beginning.

shape crown

NOTE: Change to the larger double-pointed needles when the number of stitches has been sufficiently decreased.

Round 1: *K6, k2tog; repeat from * around—63 (70, 77) stitches.

Round 2: Knit.

Round 3: *K5, k2tog; repeat from * around—54 (60, 66) stitches.

Round 4: Knit.

Round 5: *K4, k2tog; repeat from * around—45 (50, 55) stitches.

Round 6: Knit.

Round 7: *K3, k2tog; repeat from * around—36 (40, 44) stitches.

Round 8: Knit.

Sydney the Koala Bear

(shown on page 19)

SIZES

3 years (4–5 years, 6–7 years)

FINISHED MEASUREMENTS

hat circumference: 16 (18, 20)" (40.5 [45.5, 51]cm)

mitten length: 5½ (7, 9½)" (14 [18, 24]cm)

circumference: 5½ (6½, 8)" (14 [16.5, 20.5]cm)

MATERIALS

- 4 skeins Bloomingdale Farm Angoras Natural Angora 100% Angora Rabbit Fur (1 oz [30g], 35 yd [32m]), Light Gray

  (4) **medium**

- Size 7 (4.5mm) 16" (40cm) circular needle
- Size 7 (4.5mm) double-pointed needles, set of 5
- Size 5 (3.75mm) double-pointed needles, set of 5
- Stitch markers
- Stitch holder (for Medium and Large mittens only)
- 2 brown animal (crystal) eyes, ½" (13mm) in diameter
- Small amount of black felt fabric
- Craft glue
- Yarn needle

GAUGE

16 stitches and 24 rows = 4" (10cm) in stockinette stitch worked with a circular needle.

NOTE

The instructions are written for the smallest size, with changes for larger sizes in parentheses. For ease in working, circle all numbers pertaining to your size.

HAT

Using the circular needle, cast on 64 (72, 80) stitches. Join, being careful not to twist the stitches. Place a marker for the beginning of the round. Work in stockinette stitch (knit every round) until the piece measures 4½ (5, 5½)" (11.5 [12.5, 14]cm) from the beginning.

shape crown

NOTE: Change to larger double-pointed needles when the number of stitches has been sufficiently decreased.

Round 1: *K5, k2tog; repeat from * around—54 (60, 66) stitches.

Round 2: Knit.

Round 3: *K4, k2tog; repeat from * around—45 (50, 55) stitches.

Round 4: Knit.

Round 5: *K3, k2tog; repeat from * around—36 (40, 44) stitches.

Round 6: Knit.

Round 7: *K2, k2tog; repeat from * around—27 (30, 33) stitches.

Round 8: Knit.

Round 9: *K1, k2tog; repeat from * around—18 (20, 22) stitches.

shape top

Round 1: *K2, k2tog; repeat from * around—18 stitches.

Round 2: Knit.

Round 3: *K1, k2tog; repeat from * around—12 stitches.

Round 4: Knit.

Round 5: *K2tog; repeat from * around—6 stitches.

Round 6: Knit.

Round 7: *K2tog; repeat from * around—3 stitches.

Cut the yarn, leaving a long end. Use the yarn needle to thread the end through the remaining stitches. Draw together tightly and fasten off.

FOR SIZES MEDIUM (Large)

Using the smaller double-pointed needles, cast on 30 (36) stitches. Divide the stitches evenly onto 4 needles. Join, being careful not to twist the stitches. Place a marker for the beginning of the round.

wrist ribbing

Work in k1, p1 rib for 2 (3)" (5 [7.5]cm).

lower hand

Change to the larger double-pointed needles.

Rounds 1–3 (5): Knit.

shape thumb gusset

Round 1: K14 (17), place a marker, increase in each of the next 2 stitches, place a marker, k to the end of the round—32 (38) stitches.

Round 2: Knit.

Round 3: K to the marker, slip marker, increase in the next stitch, k to 1 stitch before the next marker, increase in the next stitch, slip marker, k to the end of the round—34 (40) stitches.

Round 4: Knit.

Rounds 5–6 (8): Repeat the last 2 rounds 1 (2) time(s)—36 (44) stitches, with 8 (10) stitches between markers. Slip the stitches between the markers to a holder for the thumb.

Round 7 (9): Knit, casting on 2 stitches over the stitches on the holder—30 (36) stitches.

upper hand

Knit rounds until the piece measures 2 (3)" (5 [7.5]cm) above the thumb gusset.

shape top

Round 1: *K4, k2tog; repeat from * around—25 (30) stitches.

Round 2: Knit.

Round 3: *K3, k2tog; repeat from * around—20 (24) stitches.

Round 4: Knit.

Round 5: *K2, k2tog; repeat from * around—15 (18) stitches.

Round 6: Knit.

Round 7: *K1, k2tog; repeat from * around—10 (12) stitches.

Round 8: Knit.

Round 9: *K2tog; repeat from * around—5 (6) stitches.

Cut the yarn, leaving a long end. Use the yarn needle to thread the end through the remaining stitches. Draw together tightly and fasten off.

thumb

Slip the thumb stitches from the holder back to 1 larger double-pointed needle. Join yarn and cast on 4 stitches—12 (14) stitches. Work back and forth on 2 double-pointed needles in stockinette stitch (knit on right side, purl on wrong side) until the thumb measures 1½ (2)" (3.5 [5]cm) from the last row of the thumb gusset, ending with a wrong-side row.

Next row: K2tog across—6 (7) stitches. Cut the yarn, leaving a long end. Use the yarn needle to thread the end through the remaining stitches. Draw together tightly and fasten off.

EAR (make 4 for Mittens with Embroidered Detail)

Using the larger double-pointed needles, cast on 10 stitches. Divide the stitches onto 4 needles. Join, being careful not to twist the stitches. Place a marker for the beginning of the round.

Rounds 1–5: Knit.

Round 6: K2tog around—5 stitches.

Cut the yarn, leaving a long end. Use the yarn needle to thread the end through the remaining stitches. Draw together tightly and fasten off.

EAR (make 4 for Mittens without Embroidered Detail)

Using the larger double-pointed needles, cast on 14 stitches. Divide the stitches onto 4 needles. Join, being careful not to twist the stitches. Place a marker for the beginning of the round.

Rounds 1–2: Knit.

Round 3: K2tog, k1, ssk, k2, k2tog, k1, ssk, k2—10 stitches.

Round 4: Knit.

Round 5: K2tog, k1, ssk, k2tog, k1, ssk—6 stitches.

Cut the yarn, leaving a long end. Divide the remaining stitches onto 2 needles—3 stitches per needle. Hold the needles parallel to each other and use the end to graft the stitches together.

FINISHING

Sew the cast-on edges of 2 Ears to the back of each Mitten, leaving space for the face embroidery if desired.

(Optional) Embroider face details near the end of the Mitten, below the Ears, with features facing away from the cuff edge, as follows:

With the black yarn, embroider a straight-stitch nose, a straight-stitch line down from the nose, then a small smile.

With the black yarn, embroider straight-stitch eyes.

With the white yarn, embroider 2 straight stitches for teeth, centered below the mouth.

Weave in ends.

Henry the Hippo

(shown on page 17)

SIZES

3 years (4–5 years, 6–7 years)

FINISHED MEASUREMENTS

hat circumference: 16 (18, 20)" (40.5 [45.5, 51]cm)

MATERIALS

- 1 skein each Brown Sheep Lamb's Pride Worsted, 85% wool, 15% mohair (4 oz [113.5g], 190 yd [173.5m]), #M100 Supreme Purple (A) and #M110 Orange You Glad (B) 🧶 medium
- Size 7 (4.5mm) 16" (40cm) circular needle
- Size 7 (4.5mm) double-pointed needles, set of 5
- Stitch markers
- Yarn needle
- 2 wiggle eyes, 1" (25mm) diameter
- Craft glue
- Small amount black worsted-weight yarn

GAUGE

18 stitches and 25 rows = 4" (10cm) in stockinette stitch worked with a circular needle.

NOTE

The instructions are written for the smallest size, with changes for larger sizes in parentheses. For ease in working, circle all numbers pertaining to your size.

HAT

Using a circular needle and A, cast on 72 (80, 88) stitches. Join, being careful not to twist the stitches. Place a marker for the beginning of the round. Work in stockinette stitch (knit every round) until the piece measures 4½ (5, 5½)" (11.5 [12.5, 14]cm) from the beginning.

shape crown

NOTE: Change to the double-pointed needles when the number of stitches has been sufficiently decreased.

Round 1: *K6, k2tog; repeat from * around—63 (70, 77) stitches.

Round 2: Knit.

Round 3: *K5, k2tog; repeat from * around—54 (60, 66) stitches.

Round 4: Knit.

Round 5: *K4, k2tog; repeat from * around—45 (50, 55) stitches.

Round 6: Knit.

Round 7: *K3, k2tog; repeat from * around—36 (40, 44) stitches.

Round 8: Knit.

Round 9: *K2, k2tog; repeat from * around—27 (30, 33) stitches.

Sydney the Koala Bear

(shown on page 19)

SIZES

3 years (4–5 years, 6–7 years)

FINISHED MEASUREMENTS

hat circumference: 16 (18, 20)" (40.5 [45.5, 51]cm)

mitten length: 5½ (7, 9½)" (14 [18, 24]cm)

circumference: 5½ (6½, 8)" (14 [16.5, 20.5]cm)

MATERIALS

- 4 skeins Bloomingdale Farm Angoras Natural Angora 100% Angora Rabbit Fur (1 oz [30g], 35 yd [32m]), Light Gray

  4 medium

- Size 7 (4.5mm) 16" (40cm) circular needle
- Size 7 (4.5mm) double-pointed needles, set of 5
- Size 5 (3.75mm) double-pointed needles, set of 5
- Stitch markers
- Stitch holder (for Medium and Large mittens only)
- 2 brown animal (crystal) eyes, ½" (13mm) in diameter
- Small amount of black felt fabric
- Craft glue
- Yarn needle

GAUGE

16 stitches and 24 rows = 4" (10cm) in stockinette stitch worked with a circular needle.

NOTE

The instructions are written for the smallest size, with changes for larger sizes in parentheses. For ease in working, circle all numbers pertaining to your size.

HAT

Using the circular needle, cast on 64 (72, 80) stitches. Join, being careful not to twist the stitches. Place a marker for the beginning of the round. Work in stockinette stitch (knit every round) until the piece measures 4½ (5, 5½)" (11.5 [12.5, 14]cm) from the beginning.

shape crown

NOTE: Change to larger double-pointed needles when the number of stitches has been sufficiently decreased.

Round 1: *K5, k2tog; repeat from * around—54 (60, 66) stitches.

Round 2: Knit.

Round 3: *K4, k2tog; repeat from * around—45 (50, 55) stitches.

Round 4: Knit.

Round 5: *K3, k2tog; repeat from * around—36 (40, 44) stitches.

Round 6: Knit.

Round 7: *K2, k2tog; repeat from * around—27 (30, 33) stitches.

Round 8: Knit.

Round 9: *K1, k2tog; repeat from * around—18 (20, 22) stitches.

Round 10: Knit.

Round 11: K2tog around—9 (10, 11) stitches.

Cut the yarn, leaving a long end. Use the yarn needle to thread the end through the remaining stitches. Draw together tightly and fasten off.

EAR (make 2)

Using the two larger double-pointed needles, cast on 12 stitches.

Row 1: Knit.

Row 2: Purl.

Rows 3–4: Repeat rows 1–2.

Row 5: K2tog, k to the last 2 stitches, k2tog—10 stitches.

Row 6: Purl.

Rows 7–12: Repeat the last 2 rows 3 times—4 stitches.

Row 13 (turning row): Knit.

Row 14: Purl.

Row 15: Increase in the first stitch, k to the last stitch, increase in the last stitch—6 stitches.

Row 16: Purl.

Rows 17–22: Repeat the last 2 rows 3 times—12 stitches.

Row 23: Knit.

Row 24: Purl.

Row 25: Knit.

Bind off.

FINISHING

Fold both Ears in half along the turning row and seam the sides. Sew the Ears to the top of the Hat.

Snap off the shank on the back of the eyes. Glue the eyes, centered, to the front of the Hat.

Cut a 1¼ x 1" (3 x 2.5cm) rectangle from the black felt for nose. Trim the corners to round them slightly. Glue the nose below the eyes.

Weave in ends.

MITTENS (make 2)
FOR SIZE SMALL ONLY

Using the smaller double-pointed needles, cast on 24 stitches.

Divide stitches evenly onto 4 needles— 6 stitches per needle. Join, being careful not to twist the stitches. Place a marker for the beginning of the round.

wrist ribbing

Work in k1, p1 rib for 1½" (3.8cm).

hand

Change to the larger double-pointed needles and work in stockinette stitch until the piece measures 4½" (11.5cm) from the beginning.

shape top

Round 1: *K2, k2tog; repeat from * around—18 stitches.

Round 2: Knit.

Round 3: *K1, k2tog; repeat from * around—12 stitches.

Round 4: Knit.

Round 5: *K2tog; repeat from * around—6 stitches.

Round 6: Knit.

Round 7: *K2tog; repeat from * around—3 stitches.

Cut the yarn, leaving a long end. Use the yarn needle to thread the end through the remaining stitches. Draw together tightly and fasten off.

FOR SIZES MEDIUM (LARGE)

Using smaller double-pointed needles, cast on 30 (36) stitches. Divide stitches evenly onto 4 needles. Join, being careful not to twist the stitches. Place a marker for the beginning of the round.

wrist ribbing

Work in k1, p1 rib for 2 (3)" (5 [7.5]cm).

lower hand

Change to the larger double-pointed needles.

Rounds 1–3 (5): Knit.

shape thumb gusset

Round 1: K14 (17), place a marker, increase in each of the next 2 stitches, place a marker, k to the end of the round—32 (38) stitches.

Round 2: Knit.

Round 3: K to the next marker, slip marker, increase in the next stitch, k to 1 stitch before the next marker, increase in the next stitch, slip marker, k to the end of the round—34 (40) stitches.

Round 4: Knit.

Rounds 5-6 (8): Repeat last 2 rounds 1 (2) time(s)—36 (44) stitches, with 8 (10) stitches between markers. Slip the stitches between the markers to a holder for the thumb.

Round 7 (9): Knit, casting on 2 stitches over the stitches on the holder—30 (36) stitches.

upper hand

Knit rounds until the piece measures 2 (3)" (5 [7.5]cm) above the thumb gusset.

shape top

Round 1: *K4, k2tog; repeat from * around—25 (30) stitches.

Round 2: Knit.

Round 3: *K3, k2tog; repeat from * around—20 (24) stitches.

Round 4: Knit.

Round 5: *K2, k2tog; repeat from * around—15 (18) stitches.

Round 6: Knit.

Round 7: *K1, k2tog; repeat from * around—10 (12) stitches.

Round 8: Knit.

Round 9: *K2tog; repeat from * around—5 (6) stitches.

Cut the yarn, leaving a long end. Use the yarn needle to thread the end through the remaining stitches. Draw together tightly and fasten off.

thumb

Slip the thumb stitches from the holder back to 1 larger double-pointed needle. Join yarn and cast on 4 stitches—12 (14) stitches. Work back and forth on 2 double-pointed needles in stockinette stitch (knit on right side, purl on wrong side) until the thumb measures 1½ (2)" (3.8 [5]cm) from the last row of the thumb gusset, ending with a wrong-side row.

Next row: K2tog across—6 (7) stitches. Cut the yarn, leaving a long end. Use the yarn needle to thread the end through the remaining stitches. Draw together tightly and fasten off.

FINISHING

Sew the thumb seam on the Medium and Large Mittens. Weave in ends.

Boing the Bunny

(shown on page 20)

SIZES

3 years (4–5 years, 6–7 years)

FINISHED MEASUREMENTS

scarf: 5 x 21 (25, 29)" (12.5 x 53.5 [63.5, 74]cm)

hat circumference: 16 (18, 20)" (40.5 [45.5, 51]cm)

mitten length: 5½ (7, 9½)" (14 [18, 24]cm)

circumference: 5½ (6½, 8)" (14 [16.5, 20.5]cm)

MATERIALS

- 2 skeins Brown Sheep Lamb's Pride Worsted, 85% wool, 15% mohair (4 oz [113.5g], 190 yd [173.5m]), #M34 Victorian Pink ④ **medium**
- Small amounts dark pink, black, and white worsted-weight yarn

- Size 7 (4.5mm) 16" (40cm) circular needle
- Size 7 (4.5mm) double-pointed needles, set of 5
- Size 5 (3.75mm) double-pointed needles, set of 5
- Stitch markers
- Stitch holder (for Medium and Large mittens only)
- Yarn needle

GAUGE

18 stitches and 25 rows = 4" (10cm) in stockinette stitch worked with a circular needle.

NOTE

Instructions are written for smallest size. Changes for larger sizes are in parentheses. For ease in working, circle all numbers pertaining to your size.

HAT

Using the circular needle, cast on 72 (80, 88) stitches. Join, being careful not to twist the stitches. Place a marker for the beginning of the round. Work in stockinette stitch (knit every round) until the piece measures 4½ (5, 5½)" (11.5 [12.5, 14]cm) from the beginning.

shape crown

NOTE: Change to the larger double-pointed needles when the number of stitches has been sufficiently decreased.

Round 1: *K6, k2tog; repeat from * around—63 (70, 77) stitches.

Round 2: Knit.

Round 3: *K5, k2tog; repeat from *

around—54 (60, 66) stitches.

Round 4: Knit.

Round 5: *K4, k2tog; repeat from * around—45 (50, 55) stitches.

Round 6: Knit.

Round 7: *K3, k2tog; repeat from * around—36 (40, 44) stitches.

Round 8: Knit.

Round 9: *K2, k2tog; repeat from * around—27 (30, 33) stitches.

Round 10: Knit.

Round 11: *K1, k2tog; repeat from * around—18 (20, 22) stitches.

Round 12: Knit.

Round 13: K2tog around—9 (10, 11) stitches.

Cut the yarn, leaving a long end. Use the yarn needle to thread the end through the remaining stitches. Draw together tightly and fasten off.

EAR (make 2)

Using the larger double-pointed needles, cast on 14 stitches. Divide the stitches onto 4 needles. Join, being careful not to twist the stitches. Place a marker for the beginning of the round.

Round 1: Knit.

Round 2: K6, slip the next stitch, k6, slip the last stitch.

Repeat the last 2 rounds until the piece measures 7½" (19cm) from the beginning.

Next round: K2tog, k2, k2tog, slip the next stitch, k2tog, k2, k2tog, slip the last stitch—10 stitches.

Next round: Knit.

Next round: K2tog twice, slip the next stitch, k2tog twice, slip the last stitch—6 stitches. Bind off.

Flatten the ear with the slipped stitches at the sides. Sew the bound-off edge together.

FINISHING

Sew the Ears to the sides of the Hat. With the dark pink yarn, embroider a straight-stitch triangle for the nose. With the black yarn, embroider a straight-stitch line down from the nose, then a small smile. With the black yarn, embroider straight-stitch eyelids. Weave in ends.

SCARF

NOTE: The Scarf is worked back and forth in rows on a circular needle. Using the circular needle, cast on 23 stitches.

Rows 1–6: *K1, p1; repeat from * across, ending k1.

Row 7: (K1, p1) twice, k to the last 4 stitches, (p1, k1) twice.

Row 8: (K1, p1) twice, k1, p to the last 5 stitches, k1, (p1, k1) twice.

Repeat the last 2 rows until the piece measures 21 (25, 29)" (53.5 [63.5, 74]cm) from the beginning.

Last 6 rows: Repeat rows 1–6.

Bind off.

FINISHING

Weave in ends.

MITTENS (make 2)
FOR SIZE SMALL ONLY

Using the smaller double-pointed needles, cast on 24 stitches. Divide the stitches evenly onto 4 needles—6 stitches per needle. Join, being careful not to twist the stitches. Place a marker for the beginning of the round.

wrist ribbing

Work in k1, p1 rib for 1½" (3.8cm).

hand

Change to the larger double-pointed needles and work in stockinette stitch until the piece measures 4½" (11.5cm) from the beginning.

shape top

Round 1: *K2, k2tog; repeat from * around—18 stitches.

Round 2: Knit.

Round 3: *K1, k2tog; repeat from * around—12 stitches.

Round 4: Knit.

Round 5: *K2tog; repeat from * around—6 stitches.

Round 6: Knit.

Round 7: *K2tog; repeat from * around—3 stitches.

Cut the yarn, leaving a long end. Use the yarn needle to thread the end through the remaining stitches. Draw together tightly and fasten off.

FOR SIZES MEDIUM (LARGE)

With the smaller double-pointed needles, cast on 30 (36) stitches. Divide the stitches evenly onto 4 needles. Join, being careful not to twist the stitches. Place a marker for the beginning of the round.

wrist ribbing

Work in k1, p1 rib for 2 (3)" (5 [7.5]cm).

lower hand

Change to the larger double-pointed needles.

Rounds 1–3 (5): Knit.

shape thumb gusset

Round 1: K14 (17), place a marker, increase in each of the next 2 stitches, place a marker, k to the end of the round—32 (38) stitches.

Round 2: Knit.

Round 3: K to the next marker, slip marker, increase in the next stitch, k to 1 stitch before the next marker, increase in the next stitch, slip marker, k to the end of the round—34 (40) stitches.

Round 4: Knit.

Rounds 5–6 (8): Repeat the last 2 rounds 1 (2) time(s)—36 (44) stitches, with 8 (10) stitches between the markers. Slip the stitches between the markers to a holder for the thumb.

Round 7 (9): Knit, casting on 2 stitches over the stitches on the holder—30 (36) stitches.

upper hand

Knit rounds until the piece measures 2 (3)" (5 [7.5]cm) above the thumb gusset.

shape top

Round 1: *K4, k2tog; repeat from * around—25 (30) stitches.

Round 2: Knit.

Round 3: *K3, k2tog; repeat from * around—20 (24) stitches.

Round 4: Knit.

Round 5: *K2, k2tog; repeat from * around—15 (18) stitches.

Round 6: Knit.

Round 7: *K1, k2tog; repeat from * around—10 (12) stitches.

Round 8: Knit.

Round 9: *K2tog; repeat from * around—5 (6) stitches.

Cut the yarn, leaving a long end. Use the yarn needle to thread the end through the remaining stitches. Draw together tightly and fasten off.

thumb

Slip the thumb stitches from the holder back to 1 larger double-pointed needle. Join yarn and cast on 4 stitches—12 (14) stitches. Work back and forth on 2 double-pointed needles in stockinette stitch (knit on right side, purl on wrong side) until the thumb measures 1½ (2)" (3.8 [5]cm) from the last row of the thumb gusset, ending with a wrong-side row.

Next row: K2tog across—6 (7) stitches. Cut the yarn, leaving a long end. Use the yarn needle to thread the end through the remaining stitches. Draw together tightly and fasten off.

EAR (make 4)

With the larger double-pointed needles, cast on 12 stitches. Divide the stitches onto 4 needles. Join, being careful not to twist the stitches. Place a marker for the beginning of the round.

Round 1: Knit.

Round 2: K5, slip the next stitch, k5, slip the last stitch.

Repeat the last 2 rounds until the piece measures 2" (5 cm) from the beginning.

Next round: K3, slip 1, k2tog, pass slip stitch over, k3, k2tog, slip 1, pass slip stitch over—8 stitches.

Next round: Knit.

Next round: K1, slip 1, k2tog, pass slip stitch over, k1, k2tog, slip 1, pass slip stitch over—4 stitches.

Cut the yarn, leaving a long end. Use the yarn needle to thread the end through the remaining stitches. Draw together tightly and fasten off.

Flatten the Ear with the slipped stitches at the sides. Sew bound-off edge together.

FINISHING

Sew the thumb seam on the Medium and Large Mittens.

Sew 2 Ears to the back of each mitten, leaving space to embroider the face details below the Ears.

Embroider the face details near the wrist, with features facing away from the cuff edge.

With the black yarn, embroider a straight-stitch nose, a straight-stitch line down from the nose, and then a small smile.

With the black yarn, embroider straight-stitch eyes and 3 whiskers on each side of the nose.

With the white yarn, embroider 2 straight stitches for teeth, centered below the mouth.

Weave in ends.

Minky the Cat

(shown on page 21)

SIZES

3 years (4–5 years, 6–7 years)

FINISHED MEASUREMENTS

hat circumference: 16 (18, 20)" (40.5 [45.5, 51]cm)

MATERIALS

· 1 ball each Paton's Classic Wool, 100% merino wool (4 oz [113.5g], 223 yd [204m]), #226 Black (A) and #202 Aran (B)

4 medium

· Size 7 (4.5mm) 16" (40cm) circular needle
· Size 7 (4.5mm) double-pointed needles, set of 5
· Stitch markers
· Yarn needle
· 2 blue buttons, ⅝" (16mm) in diameter

GAUGE

18 stitches and 25 rows = 4" (10cm) in stockinette stitch worked with a circular needle.

NOTE The instructions are written for the smallest size. Changes for the larger sizes are in parentheses. For ease in working, circle all numbers pertaining to your size.

PATTERN STITCH

SEED STITCH (worked in the round)

Round 1: *K1, p1; repeat from * around.

Round 2: Purl the knit stitches, and knit the purl stitches.

Repeat round 2 for seed stitch pattern.

HAT

Using the circular needle and A, cast on 72 (80, 88) stitches. Join, being careful not to twist the stitches. Place a marker for the beginning of the round.

Rounds 1–10: Knit.

Change to B and work in seed stitch until the piece measures 4½ (5, 5½)" (11.5 [12.5, 14]cm) from the beginning.

shape crown

NOTE: Change to the double-pointed needles when the number of stitches has been sufficiently decreased.

Round 1: *Work in seed stitch as established for 6 stitches, k2tog; repeat from * around—63 (70, 77) stitches.

Round 2: Work in seed stitch as established.

Round 3: *Work in seed stitch as established for 5 stitches, k2tog; repeat from * around—54 (60, 66) stitches.

Round 4: Work in seed stitch as established.

Round 5: *Work in seed stitch as established for 4 stitches, k2tog; repeat from * around—45 (50, 55) stitches.

Round 6: Work in seed stitch as established.

Round 7: *Work in seed stitch as established for 3 stitches, k2tog; repeat from * around—36 (40, 44) stitches.

Round 8: Work in seed stitch as established.

Round 9: *K2, k2tog; repeat from * around—27 (30, 33) stitches.

Round 10: Knit.

Round 11: *K1, k2tog; repeat from * around—18 (20, 22) stitches.

Round 12: Knit.

Round 13: K2tog around—9 (10, 11) stitches.

Cut the yarn, leaving a long end. Use the yarn needle to thread the end through the remaining stitches. Draw together tightly. Sew seam and fasten off.

EAR (make 4)

Using the double-pointed needles and A, cast on 11 stitches.

Row 1: Knit.

Row 2: P2tog, p to the end of the row—10 stitches.

Row 3: K2tog, k to the end of the row—9 stitches.

Rows 4–11: Repeat last 2 rows 4 times—1 stitch. Fasten off.

FINISHING

Sew the Ears together in pairs. Sew the ears to the top of the Hat. Sew the buttons to the front of the Hat for eyes. Using A, embroider a straight-stitch nose below the eyes. With A, embroider 3 long stitches on each side of the nose for the whiskers. Weave in ends.

Blizzard the Polar Bear

(shown on page 22)

SIZES

3 years (4–5 years, 6–7 years)

FINISHED MEASUREMENTS

scarf: 5 x 21 (25, 29)" (12.5 x 53.5 [63.5, 74]cm)

hat circumference: 16 (18, 20)" (40.5 [45.5, 51]cm)

MATERIALS

- 2 skeins Brown Sheep Lamb's Pride Worsted, 85% wool, 15% mohair (4 oz [113.5g], 190 yd [173.5m]), #M11 White Frost 🌀 **medium**
- Size 7 (4.5mm) 16" (40cm) circular needle
- Size 7 (4.5mm) double-pointed needles, set of 5
- Stitch markers
- Yarn needle
- 2 black buttons, ½" (13mm) in diameter
- 1 black pom-pom, 1" (25mm) in diameter

GAUGE

18 stitches and 25 rows = 4" (10cm) in stockinette stitch worked with a circular needle.

NOTE

The instructions are written for the smallest size. Changes for the larger sizes are in parentheses. For ease in working, circle all numbers pertaining to your size.

HAT

Using the circular needle, cast on 72 (80, 88) stitches. Join, being careful not to twist the stitches. Place a marker for the beginning of the round. Work in stockinette stitch (knit every round) until the piece measures 4½ (5, 5½)" (11.5 [12.5, 14]cm) from the beginning.

shape crown

NOTE: Change to the larger double-pointed needles when the number of stitches is sufficiently decreased.

Round 1: *K6, k2tog; repeat from * around—63 (70, 77) stitches.

Round 2: Knit.

Round 3: *K5, k2tog; repeat from * around—54 (60, 66) stitches.

Round 4: Knit.

Round 5: *K4, k2tog; repeat from * around—45 (50, 55) stitches.

Round 6: Knit.

Round 7: *K3, k2tog; repeat from * around—36 (40, 44) stitches.

Round 8: Knit.

Round 9: *K2, k2tog; repeat from * around—27 (30, 33) stitches.

Round 10: Knit.

Round 11: *K1, k2tog; repeat from * around—18 (20, 22) stitches.

Round 12: Knit.

Round 13: K2tog around—9 (10, 11) stitches.

Cut the yarn, leaving a long end. Use the yarn needle to thread the end through the remaining stitches. Draw together tightly and fasten off.

EAR (make 2)

Using the larger double-pointed needles, cast on 20 stitches. Divide the stitches onto 4 needles—5 stitches per needle. Join, being careful not to twist the stitches. Place a marker for the beginning of the round.

Rounds 1–4: Knit.

Round 5: On the first needle, k2tog, k to the end of the needle; on the second needle, k to the last 2 stitches, k2tog; on the third needle, k2tog, k to the end of the needle; on the fourth needle, k to the last 2 stitches, k2tog—4 stitches on each needle.

Rounds 6–7: Repeat round 5 twice—2 stitches remain on each needle. Slip stitches from the first and second needles onto the first needle; slip stitches from the third and fourth needles onto the third needle. Cut the yarn, leaving a long end. Hold the first and third needles parallel to each other and use the end to graft the stitches together.

FINISHING

Stuff the Ear with about 60" (152.5cm) of matching yarn. Sew the Ears to the top of the Hat. Sew black buttons to the front of the Hat for the eyes. Sew the pom-pom to the front of the Hat for the nose.

Weave in ends.

Cheddar the Mouse

(shown on page 23)

SIZES

3 years (4–5 years, 6–7 years)

FINISHED MEASUREMENTS

hat circumference: 16 (18, 20)" (40.5 [45.5, 51]cm)

MATERIALS

- 1 skein each Paton's Classic Wool, 100% merino wool (3½ oz [100g], 223 yd [205m]), #231 Chestnut Brown (A) and #225 Dark Grey Mix (B) **(4) medium**
- Size 7 (4.5mm) 16" (40cm) circular needle
- Size 7 (4.5mm) double-pointed needles, set of 5
- Size 5 (3.75mm) double-pointed needles, set of 5
- Stitch markers
- Small amount of polyester fiberfill stuffing
- 2 dark brown buttons, ¼" (6mm) in diameter
- 7 brown pom-poms, 1" (25mm) in diameter
- Yarn needle

GAUGE

18 stitches and 25 rows = 4" (10cm) in stockinette stitch worked with a circular needle.

NOTE

The instructions are written for the smallest size. Changes for the larger sizes are in parentheses. For ease in working, circle all numbers pertaining to your size.

HAT

Using the circular needle and A, cast on 72 (80, 88) stitches. Join, being careful not to twist the stitches. Place a marker for the beginning of the round. Work in stockinette stitch (knit every round) until the piece measures 4½ (5, 5½)" (11.5 [12.5, 14]cm) from the beginning.

shape crown

NOTE: Change to larger double-pointed needles when the number of stitches has been sufficiently decreased.

Round 1: *K6, k2tog; repeat from * around—63 (70, 77) stitches.

Round 2: Knit.

Round 3: *K5, k2tog; repeat from * around—54 (60, 66) stitches.

Round 4: Knit.

Round 5: *K4, k2tog; repeat from * around—45 (50, 55) stitches.

Round 6: Knit.

Round 7: *K3, k2tog; repeat from * around—36 (40, 44) stitches.

Round 8: Knit.

Round 9: *K2, k2tog; repeat from * around—27 (30, 33) stitches.

Round 10: Knit.

Round 11: *K1, k2tog; repeat from * around—18 (20, 22) stitches.

Round 12: Knit.

Round 13: K2tog around—9 (10, 11) stitches.

Cut the yarn, leaving a long end. Use the yarn needle to thread the end through the remaining stitches. Draw together tightly and fasten off.

OUTER EAR (make 2)

Using the larger double-pointed needles and A, cast on 16 stitches. Divide the stitches evenly onto 4 needles—4 stitches per needle. Join, being careful not to twist the stitches. Place a marker for the beginning of the round.

Rounds 1–3: Knit.

Round 4: Increase 1 stitch on each needle—20 stitches.

Rounds 5–9: Knit.

Round 10: On the first needle, k2tog, k to the end of the needle; on the second needle, k to the last 2 stitches, k2tog; on the third needle, k2tog, k to the end of the needle; on the fourth needle, k to the last 2 stitches, k2tog—4 stitches on each needle.

Rounds 11–12: Repeat round 10 twice—2 stitches remain on each needle.

Slip stitches from the first and second needles onto the first needle; slip stitches from the third and fourth needles onto the third needle. Cut the yarn, leaving a long end. Hold the first and third needles parallel to each other and use the end to graft the stitches together.

INNER EAR (make 2)

Using 2 larger double-pointed needles and B, cast on 8 stitches.

Rows 1–5: Knit.

Rows 6–7: K2tog, k to the last 2 stitches, k2tog—4 stitches.

Bind off.

FINISHING

Sew an Inner Ear to each Outer Ear, working through the front layer of the Outer Ear only.

Stuff the ears lightly and sew them to the top of the Hat.

Sew the buttons to the front of the Hat for eyes.

Sew the pom-pom to the front of the Hat for the nose.

Cut 4 strands of B, each 6" (15cm) long. Using the yarn needle, weave the strands behind the pom-pom nose, leaving the ends of the strands extending evenly on each side of the nose for whiskers. Trim the strands evenly.

Weave in ends.

02 | Easy

Quacker the Duck

Everyone will go "quackers" for this cheerful set. The bill is knit flat in pieces and stuffed—it even does double-duty as a visor. No more sun in your little duckling's eyes!

Instructions on page 53.

Calypso the Whale

Thar she blows! The spout on this charming whale hat is easily constructed—simply cast on and immediately bind off the stitches. Then form the strip into four loops and sew to the crown of the hat. Store-bought animal eyes, simple embroidery, and a scarf with pockets complete the look.

Instructions on page 56.

Bandit the Raccoon

Knit this playful, masked creature in soft wool and mohair yarn. The easy stripe on the ends of the scarf gives the look of a tail. Perky, pointed ears on the hat and mittens are knit flat and sewn together, while the nose is embroidered with a simple straight stitch.

Instructions on page 60.

Rory the Lion

The king of the jungle is easy to craft—making his mane is
as simple as adding fringe. His ears are knit in the round and stuffed.
Use a store-bought pom-pom for his nose or make your own.

Instructions on page 63.

Whinny the Horse

There's no horsing around with this fun set. Making the luxurious mane is as easy as adding fringe.

The ears are knit flat and sewn together. Long fringe on the scarf keeps the look wild and woolly!

Instructions on page 66.

Truffles the Cat

This cheerful kitty-cat set will tickle kids pink with its sweet embroidered hat and mittens.
The hat is knit in the round on circular and double-pointed needles and the ears are knit flat.

Instructions on page 68.

Quacker the Duck

(shown on page 47)

SIZES

3 years (4–5 years, 6–7 years)

FINISHED MEASUREMENTS

hat circumference: 16 (18, 20)" (40.5 [45.5, 51]cm)

scarf: 5 x 21 (25, 29)" (12.5 x 53.5 [63.5, 74]cm)

mitten length: 5½ (7, 9½)" (14 [18, 24]cm)

circumference: 5½ (6½, 8)" (14 [16.5, 20.5]cm)

MATERIALS

- 2 skeins Brown Sheep Lamb's Pride Worsted, 85% wool, 15% mohair (4 oz [113.5g], 190 yd [173.5m]), #M155 Lemon Drop (A), and 1 skein #M110 Orange You Glad (B) ④ **medium**
- Small amount black worsted-weight yarn
- Size 7 (4.5mm) 16" (40cm) circular needle
- Size 5 (3.75mm) knitting needles
- Size 7 (4.5mm) double-pointed needles, set of 5
- Size 5 (3.75mm) double-pointed needles, set of 5
- Stitch markers
- Stitch holder (for Medium and Large mittens only)
- 2 black buttons, ¼" (6mm) in diameter
- Small amount of polyester fiberfill stuffing
- Yarn needle

GAUGE

18 stitches and 25 rows = 4" (10cm) in stockinette stitch worked with a circular needle.

NOTE

The instructions are written for the smallest size. Changes for the larger sizes are in parentheses. For ease in working, circle all numbers pertaining to your size.

HAT

Using the circular needle, cast on 72 (80, 88) stitches. Join, being careful not to twist the stitches. Place a marker for the beginning of the round. Work in stockinette stitch (knit every round) until piece measures 4½ (5, 5½)" (11.5 [12.5, 14]cm) from the beginning.

shape crown

NOTE: Change to the larger double-pointed needles when the number of stitches has been sufficiently decreased.

Round 1: *K6, k2tog; repeat from * around—63 (70, 77) stitches.

Round 2: Knit.

Round 3: *K5, k2tog; repeat from * around—54 (60, 66) stitches.

Round 4: Knit.

Round 5: *K4, k2tog; repeat from * around—45 (50, 55) stitches.

Round 6: Knit.

Round 7: *K3, k2tog; repeat from * around—36 (40, 44) stitches.

Round 8: Knit.

Round 9: *K2, k2tog; repeat from * around—27 (30, 33) stitches.

Round 10: Knit.

Round 11: *K1, k2tog; repeat from * around—18 (20, 22) stitches.

Round 12: Knit.

Round 13: K2tog around—9 (10, 11) stitches.

Cut the yarn, leaving a long end. Use the yarn needle to thread the end through the remaining stitches. Draw together tightly and fasten off.

BILL (make 2)

Using the circular needle and B, cast on 18 stitches. Work back and forth on the circular needle as if working on straight needles.

Row 1: Knit.

Row 2: Purl.

Rows 3–4: Repeat rows 1–2.

Row 5: K2tog, k to the last 2 stitches, k2tog—16 stitches.

Row 6: P2tog, p to the last 2 stitches, p2tog—14 stitches.

Rows 7–10: Repeat rows 5–6 twice— 6 stitches.

Bind off.

FINISHING

Sew the Bill pieces together along the bound-off edges and the decreased side edges. Stuff the Bill lightly and sew the cast-on edge to the front of the Hat. Sew the buttons to the front of the Hat for eyes.

Weave in ends.

SCARF

Using the straight needles and A, cast on 34 stitches.

Row 1: *K1, p1; repeat from * across.

Repeat the last row (k1, p1 rib) until the piece measures 10½ (12½, 14½)" (27 [32, 37]cm) from the beginning. Change to B and continue in k1, p1 rib until the piece measures 21 (25, 29)" (53.5 [63.5, 74]cm) from the beginning. Bind off.

FINISHING

Weave in ends.

MITTENS (make 2)

FOR SIZE SMALL ONLY

Using the smaller double-pointed needles and A, cast on 24 stitches. Divide the stitches evenly onto 4 needles—6 stitches per needle.

Join, being careful not to twist the stitches. Place a marker for the beginning of the round.

wrist ribbing

Work in k1, p1 rib for 1½" (3.8cm).

hand

Change to the larger double-pointed needles and work in stockinette stitch (knit every round) until the piece measures 4½" (11.5cm) from the beginning.

shape top

Round 1: *K2, k2tog; repeat from * around—18 stitches.

Round 2: Knit.

Round 3: *K1, k2tog; repeat from * around—12 stitches.

Round 4: Knit.

Round 5: *K2tog; repeat from * around—6 stitches.

Round 6: Knit.

Round 7: *K2tog; repeat from * around—3 stitches.

Cut the yarn, leaving a long end. Use the yarn needle to thread the end through the remaining stitches. Draw together tightly and fasten off.

FOR SIZES MEDIUM (LARGE)

Using the smaller double-pointed needles and A, cast on 30 (36) stitches. Divide the stitches evenly onto 4 needles. Join, being careful not to twist the stitches. Place a marker for the beginning of the round.

wrist ribbing

Work in k1, p1 rib for 2 (3)" (5 [7.5]cm).

lower hand

Change to the larger double-pointed needles.

Rounds 1–3 (5): Knit.

shape thumb gusset

Round 1: K14 (17), place a marker, increase in each of the next 2 stitches, place a marker, k to the end of the round—32 (38) stitches.

Round 2: Knit.

Round 3: K to the next marker, slip marker, increase in the next stitch, k to 1 stitch before the next marker, increase in the next stitch, slip marker, k to the end of the round—34 (40) stitches.

Round 4: Knit.

Rounds 5–6 (8): Repeat the last 2 rounds 1 (2) time(s)—36 (44) stitches, with 8 (10) stitches between the markers. Slip the stitches between the markers to a holder for the thumb.

Round 7 (9): Knit, casting on 2 stitches over the stitches on the holder—30 (36) stitches.

upper hand

Knit until the piece measures 2 (3)" (5 [7.5]cm) above the thumb gusset.

shape top

Round 1: *K4, k2tog; repeat from * around—25 (30) stitches.

Round 2: Knit.

Round 3: *K3, k2tog; repeat from * around—20 (24) stitches.

Round 4: Knit.

Round 5: *K2, k2tog; repeat from * around—15 (18) stitches.

Round 6: Knit.

Round 7: *K1, k2tog; repeat from * around—10 (12) stitches.

Round 8: Knit.

Round 9: *K2tog; repeat from * around—5 (6) stitches.

Cut the yarn, leaving a long end. Use the yarn needle to thread the end through the remaining stitches. Draw together tightly and fasten off.

thumb

Slip the thumb stitches from the holder back to 1 larger double-pointed needle. Join yarn and cast on 4 stitches—12 (14) stitches. Work back and forth on 2 double-pointed needles in stockinette stitch (knit on right side, purl on wrong side) until the thumb measures 1½ (2)" (3.5 [5]cm) from the last row of the thumb gusset, ending with a wrong-side row.

Next row: K2tog across—6 (7) stitches.

Cut the yarn, leaving a long end. Use the yarn needle to thread the end through the remaining stitches. Draw together tightly and fasten off.

BILL (make 2)

Using the 2 larger double-pointed needles and B, cast on 13 stitches.

Row 1: Purl.

Row 2: K2tog, k to last 2 stitches, k2tog—11 stitches.

Rows 3–10: Repeat last 2 rows 4 times—3 stitches.

Row 11: Slip 1, k2tog, psso.

Bind off the last stitch.

FINISHING

Sew the thumb seam on the Medium and Large Mittens.

Sew a Bill to the back of each Mitten.

With black yarn, embroider two straight-stitch eyes centered above the Bill on each Mitten.

Weave in ends.

Calypso the Whale

(shown on page 48)

SIZES

3 years (4–5 years, 6–7 years)

FINISHED MEASUREMENTS

scarf: 5 x 21 (25, 29)" (12.5 x 53.5 [63.5, 74]cm)

hat circumference: 16 (18, 20)" (40.5 [45.5, 51]cm)

mitten length: 5½ (7, 9½)" (14 [18, 24]cm)

circumference: 5½ (6½, 8)" (14 [16.5, 20.5]cm)

MATERIALS

- 2 skeins Brown Sheep Lamb's Pride Worsted, 85% wool, 15% mohair (4 oz [113.5g], 190 yd [173.5m]), #M79 Blue Boy (A), and 1 skein #M11 White Frost (B) **4** **medium**
- Small amount black worsted-weight yarn
- Size 7 (4.5mm) 16" (40cm) circular needle
- Size 7 (4.5mm) double-pointed needles, set of 5
- Size 5 (3.75mm) double-pointed needles, set of 5
- Stitch markers
- Stitch holder (for Medium and Large mittens only)
- 2 wiggle eyes, ⅜" (10mm) in diameter
- Craft glue
- Yarn needle

GAUGE

18 stitches and 25 rows = 4" (10cm) in stockinette stitch worked with a circular needle.

NOTE

The instructions are written for the smallest size, with changes for the larger sizes in parentheses. For ease in working, circle all numbers pertaining to your size.

HAT

Using the circular needle and A, cast on 72 (80, 88) stitches. Join, being careful not to twist the stitches. Place a marker for the beginning of the round. Work in stockinette stitch (knit every round) until the piece measures 4½ (5, 5½)" (11.5 [12.5, 14]cm) from the beginning.

shape crown

NOTE: Change to the larger double-pointed needles when the number of stitches has been sufficiently decreased.

Round 1: *K6, k2tog; repeat from * around—63 (70, 77) stitches.

Round 2: Knit.

Round 3: *K5, k2tog; repeat from * around—54 (60, 66) stitches.

Round 4: Knit.

Round 5: *K4, k2tog; repeat from * around—45 (50, 55) stitches.

Round 6: Knit.

Round 7: *K3, k2tog; repeat from * around—36 (40, 44) stitches.

Round 8: Knit.

Round 9: *K2, k2tog; repeat from * around—27 (30, 33) stitches.

Round 10: Knit.

Round 11: *K1, k2tog; repeat from * around—18 (20, 22) stitches.

Round 12: Knit.

Round 13: K2tog around—9 (10, 11) stitches.

Cut the yarn, leaving a long end. Use the yarn needle to thread the end through the remaining stitches. Draw together tightly and fasten off.

SPOUT

Using the larger double-pointed needles and B, cast on 34 stitches. Bind off, leaving a long end for sewing. Fold the strand into 4 loops. Use the end to tack the loops together and sew to the top of the Hat.

FINISHING

Glue the eyes to the front of the Hat. Using B, embroider a back-stitch smile just above the rolled edge. Weave in ends.

FINISHING

Embroider the whale features on the right side of each end of the Scarf, centered within the stockinette-stitch section. Using the black yarn, embroider a back-stitch smile and two eyes. Using B, embroider a back-stitch spout centered above the eyes.

To form a pocket, fold one end of the Scarf at the turning row and sew the sides to the Scarf. To form the other pocket, repeat this process on the opposite end of the Scarf.

Weave in ends.

SCARF

NOTE: The Scarf is worked back and forth in rows on a circular needle. The beginning and end of the Scarf will be folded to the right side and seamed to make the pockets.

Using the circular needle and A, cast on 23 stitches.

Rows 1–6: *K1, p1; repeat from * across, ending k1.

Row 7 (wrong side): K5, p to last 5 stitches, k5.

Row 8: Knit.

Repeat the last 2 rows until the piece measures 4" (10cm) from the beginning, ending with a right-side row.

Next 7 rows: Knit.

Next row (first turning row): Purl.

Next 7 rows: Knit.

NOTE: The right side and wrong side of the Scarf reverse at this point.

Next row (wrong side): K5, p to the last 5 stitches, k5.

Next row (right side): Knit.

Repeat the last 2 rows until the piece measures 21 (25, 29)" (53.5 [63.5, 74]cm) from the beginning, ending with a wrong-side row.

Next 7 rows: Knit.

Next row (second turning row): Purl.

Next 7 rows: Knit.

Next row (wrong side): K5, p to the last 5 stitches, k5.

Next row (right side): Knit.

Repeat the last 2 rows until the piece measures 4" (10cm) from the second turning row, and end with a right-side row.

Last 6 rows: Knit.

Bind off.

FINISHING

Embroider the whale features on the right side of each end of the Scarf, centered within the stockinette-stitch section. Using the black yarn, embroider a back-stitch smile and two eyes. Using B, embroider a back-stitch spout centered above the eyes. To form a pocket, fold one end of the Scarf at the turning row and sew the sides to the Scarf. To form the other pocket, repeat this process on the opposite end of the Scarf. Weave in ends.

MITTENS (make 2)

FOR SIZE SMALL ONLY

Using the smaller double-pointed needles and A, cast on 24 stitches. Divide the stitches evenly onto 4 needles—6 stitches per needle. Join, being careful not to twist the stitches. Place a marker for the beginning of the round.

wrist ribbing

Work in k1, p1 rib for 1½" (3.8cm).

hand

Change to the larger double-pointed needles and work in stockinette stitch (knit all rounds) until the piece measures 4½" (11.5cm) from the beginning.

shape top

Round 1: *K2, k2tog; repeat from * around—18 stitches.

Round 2: Knit.

Round 3: *K1, k2tog; repeat from * around—12 stitches.

Round 4: Knit.

Round 5: *K2tog; repeat from * around—6 stitches.

Round 6: Knit.

Round 7: *K2tog; repeat from * around—3 stitches.

Cut the yarn, leaving a long end. Use the yarn needle to thread the end through the remaining stitches. Draw together tightly and fasten off.

FOR SIZES MEDIUM (LARGE)

Using the smaller double-pointed needles and A, cast on 30 (36) stitches. Divide the stitches evenly onto 4 needles. Join, being careful not to twist the stitches. Place a marker for the beginning of the round.

wrist ribbing

Work in k1, p1 rib for 2 (3)" (5 [7.5]cm).

lower hand

Change to the larger double-pointed needles.

Rounds 1–3 (5): Knit.

shape thumb gusset

Round 1: K14 (17), place a marker, increase in each of the next 2 stitches, place a marker, k to the end of the round—32 (38) stitches.

Round 2: Knit.

Round 3: K to the next marker, slip marker, increase in the next stitch, k to 1 stitch before the next marker, increase in the next stitch, slip marker, k to the end of the round—34 (40) stitches.

Round 4: Knit.

Rounds 5–6 (8): Repeat the last 2 rounds 1 (2) time(s)—36 (44) stitches, with 8 (10) stitches between the markers. Slip the stitches between the markers to a holder for the thumb.

Round 7 (9): Knit, casting on 2 stitches over the stitches on the holder—30 (36) stitches.

upper hand

Knit rounds until the piece measures 2 (3)" (5 [7.5]cm) above the thumb gusset.

shape top

Round 1: *K4, k2tog; repeat from * around—25 (30) stitches.

Round 2: Knit.

Round 3: *K3, k2tog; repeat from * around—20 (24) stitches.

Round 4: Knit.

Round 5: *K2, k2tog; repeat from * around—15 (18) stitches.

Round 6: Knit.

Round 7: *K1, k2tog; repeat from * around—10 (12) stitches.

Round 8: Knit.

Round 9: *K2tog; repeat from *
around—5 (6) stitches.

Cut the yarn, leaving a long end. Use
the yarn needle to thread the end
through the remaining stitches. Draw
together tightly and fasten off.

thumb

Slip the thumb stitches from the
holder back to 1 larger double-pointed
needle. Join the yarn and cast on 4
stitches—12 (14) stitches. Work back
and forth on 2 double-pointed needles
in stockinette stitch (knit on right side,

purl on wrong side) until the thumb
measures 1½ (2)" (3.8 [5]cm) from the
last row of the thumb gusset, ending
with a wrong-side row.

Next row: K2tog across—6 (7) stitches.
Cut the yarn, leaving a long end. Use
the yarn needle to thread the end
through the remaining stitches. Draw
together tightly and fasten off.

FINISHING

Sew the thumb seam on the Medium
and Large Mittens.
Embroider the eyes, mouth, and

spout detail—same as on the Scarf
pocket—on the back of each Mitten,
with the features facing away from the
cuff edge.

Weave in ends.

EASY

Bandit the Raccoon

(shown on page 49)

SIZES

3 years (4–5 years, 6–7 years)

FINISHED MEASUREMENTS

scarf: 5 x 21 (25, 29)" (12.5 x 53.5 [63.5, 74]cm)

hat circumference: 16 (18, 20)" (40.5 [45.5, 51]cm)

mitten length: 5½ (7, 9½)" (14 [18, 24]cm)

circumference: 5½ (6½, 8)" (14 [16.5, 20.5]cm)

MATERIALS

- 2 skeins Brown Sheep Lamb's Pride Worsted, 85% wool, 15% mohair (4 oz [113.5g], 190 yd [173.5m]), #M03 Grey Heather (A), and 1 skein #M05 Onyx (B) **④ medium**
- Size 7 (4.5mm) 16" (40cm) circular needle
- Size 7 (4.5mm) double-pointed needles, set of 5
- Size 5 (3.75mm) double-pointed needles, set of 5
- Stitch markers
- Stitch holder (for Medium and Large mittens only)
- 2 wiggle eyes, ⅝" (16mm) in diameter
- Craft glue
- Yarn needle

GAUGE

18 stitches and 25 rows = 4" (10cm) in stockinette stitch worked with a circular needle.

NOTE

The instructions are written for the smallest size, with changes for the larger sizes in parentheses. For ease in working, circle all numbers pertaining to your size.

HAT

Using the circular needle and A, cast on 72 (80, 88) stitches. Join, being careful not to twist the stitches. Place a marker for the beginning of the round.

Rounds 1–16: Knit.

Change to B.

Rounds 17–28: Knit.

Change to A and continue in stockinette stitch (knit every round) until the piece measures 4½ (5, 5½)" (11.5 [12.5, 14]cm) from the beginning.

shape crown

NOTE: Change to larger double-pointed needles when the number of stitches has been sufficiently decreased.

Round 1: *K6, k2tog; repeat from * around—63 (70, 77) stitches.

Round 2: Knit.

Round 3: *K5, k2tog; repeat from * around—54 (60, 66) stitches.

Round 4: Knit.

Round 5: *K4, k2tog; repeat from * around—45 (50, 55) stitches.

Round 6: Knit.

Round 7: *K3, k2tog; repeat from * around—36 (40, 44) stitches.

Round 8: Knit.

Round 9: *K2, k2tog; repeat from * around—27 (30, 33) stitches.

Round 10: Knit.

Round 11: *K1, k2tog; repeat from * around—18 (20, 22) stitches.

Round 12: Knit.

Round 13: K2tog around—9 (10, 11) stitches.

Cut the yarn, leaving a long end. Use the yarn needle to thread the end through remaining stitches. Draw together tightly and fasten off.

EAR (make 4)

Using the larger double-pointed needles and A, cast on 11 stitches.

Row 1: Knit.

Row 2: P2tog, p to end of row—10 stitches.

Row 3: K2tog, k to end of row—9 stitches.

Rows 4–11: Repeat rows 2–3 four times—1 stitch.

Bind off the last stitch.

FINISHING

Sew the Ears together in pairs and sew them to the top of the Hat. Glue the wiggle eyes to the front of the Hat.

Using B, embroider a straight-stitch nose below the eyes.

Weave in ends.

SCARF

NOTE: The Scarf is worked back and forth in rows on a circular needle.

Using the circular needle and B, cast on 21 stitches.

Rows 1–10: Knit.

Change to A, and continue in garter stitch (knit every row) until the piece measures 19 (23, 27)" (48.5 [58.5, 68.5]cm) from the beginning, ending with a wrong-side row.

Change to B.

Next 10 rows: Knit.

Bind off.

FINISHING

Weave in ends.

MITTENS (make 2)

FOR SIZE SMALL ONLY

Using the smaller double-pointed needles and A, cast on 24 stitches. Divide the stitches evenly onto 4 needles. Join, being careful not to twist the stitches. Place a marker for the beginning of the round.

wrist ribbing

Work in k1, p1 rib for 1½" (3.8cm).

hand

Change to the larger double-pointed needles. Work in stockinette stitch (knit all rounds) until the piece measures 2" (5cm) from the beginning. Change to B.

Rounds 1–5: Knit.

Change to A and continue in stockinette stitch until piece measures 4½" (11.5cm) from the beginning.

shape top

Round 1: *K2, k2tog; repeat from * around—18 stitches.

Round 2: Knit.

Round 3: *K1, k2tog; repeat from * around—12 stitches.

Round 4: Knit.

Round 5: *K2tog; repeat from * around—6 stitches.

Round 6: Knit.

Round 7: *K2tog; repeat from * around—3 stitches.

Cut the yarn, leaving a long end. Use the yarn needle to thread the end through the remaining stitches. Draw together tightly and fasten off.

shape crown

NOTE: Change to the larger double-pointed needles when necessary.

Round 1: *K6, k2tog; repeat from * around—63 (70, 77) stitches.

Even-Numbered Rounds 2–12: Knit.

Round 3: *K5, k2tog; repeat from * around—54 (60, 66) stitches.

Round 5: *K4, k2tog; repeat from * around—45 (50, 55) stitches.

Round 7: *K3, k2tog; repeat from * around—36 (40, 44) stitches.

Round 9: *K2, k2tog; repeat from * around—27 (30, 33) stitches.

Round 11: *K1, k2tog; repeat from * around—18 (20, 22) stitches.

Round 13: K2tog around—9 (10, 11) stitches.

Cut the yarn, leaving a long end. Use the yarn needle to thread the end through the remaining stitches. Draw together tightly and fasten off.

EAR (make 2)

Using the larger double-pointed needles, cast on 20 stitches. Divide the stitches onto 4 needles—5 stitches per needle. Join, being careful not to twist the stitches. Place a marker for the beginning of the round.

Rounds 1–4: Knit.

Round 5: On the first needle, k2tog, k to the end of the needle; on the second needle, k to the last 2 stitches, k2tog; on the third needle, k2tog, k to the end of the needle; on the fourth needle, k to the last 2 stitches, k2tog—4 stitches on each needle.

Rounds 6–7: Repeat round 5 twice—2 stitches on each needle. Slip the stitches from the first and second needles onto the first needle; slip the stitches from the third and fourth needles onto the third needle. Cut the yarn, leaving a long end. Hold the first and third needles parallel and graft the stitches together.

FINISHING

Stuff each Ear with about 12" (30.5cm) of yarn and sew ears to top of Hat. Sew the buttons on the front of the Hat for the eyes.

Sew the pom-pom on the front of the Hat, centered below the eyes.

MANE

Cut about forty 5" (12.5cm) strands of yarn. Lay the Hat flat and mark the row along the fold at each.

Begin attaching the mane above the stockinette-stitch roll at the lower edge as follows: Fold a strand of yarn in half and, with the crochet hook, pull the folded end through the marked row. Pull the ends through the loop and tighten. Repeat this step all along the side of the Hat to the ear, and then work back down the side of the Hat. Trim the fringe ends evenly. Weave in ends.

SCARF

NOTE: The Scarf is worked back and forth in rows on the circular needle.

Using the circular needle and A, cast on 30 stitches.

Rows 1–5: *K1, p1; repeat from * across for seed stitch pattern.

Row 6: (K1, p1) twice, k to the last 4 stitches, (p1, k1) twice.

Row 7: (K1, p1) twice, k1, p to the last 5 stitches, k1, (p1, k1) twice.

Row 8: (K1, p1) twice, k1, (p2, k2, p2, k1) twice, p2, k2, p2, k1, (p1, k1) twice.

Row 9: (K1, p1) twice, k1, (k2, p2, k2, p1) twice, k2, p2, k3, (p1, k1) twice.

Repeat rows 6–9 until the piece measures 28½ (33½, 38½)" (72 [85.5, 98]cm) from the beginning.

Last 5 rows: Repeat rows 1–5.
Bind off.

FRINGE
Cut about twenty 5" (12.5cm) strands of yarn. Fold one strand in half and, with the crochet hook, pull the folded end through the end of the Scarf. Pull the ends through the loop and tighten. Attach fringe evenly spaced along each Scarf end. Trim fringe ends evenly.

FINISHING
Weave in ends.

MITTENS (make 2)
FOR SIZE SMALL ONLY
Using the smaller double-pointed needles, cast on 24 stitches. Divide the stitches evenly onto 4 needles. Join, being careful not to twist the stitches. Place a marker for the beginning of the round.
wrist ribbing
Work in k1, p1 rib for 1½" (3.8cm).
hand
Change to the larger double-pointed needles and A. Work in stockinette stitch (knit every round) until the piece measures 4½" (11.5cm).

shape top
Round 1: *K2, k2tog; repeat from * around—18 stitches.
Round 2: Knit.
Round 3: *K1, k2tog; repeat from * around—12 stitches.
Round 4: Knit.
Round 5: *K2tog; repeat from * around—6 stitches.
Round 6: Knit.
Round 7: *K2tog; repeat from * around—3 stitches.
Cut the yarn, leaving a long end. Use the yarn needle to thread the end through the remaining stitches. Draw together tightly and fasten off.

FOR SIZES MEDIUM (LARGE)
Using the smaller double-pointed needles, cast on 30 (36) stitches. Divide the stitches evenly onto 4 needles. Join, while being careful not to twist the stitches. Place a marker for the beginning of the round.
wrist ribbing
Work in k1, p1 rib for 2 (3)" (5 [7.5]cm).
lower hand
Change to the larger double-pointed needles.
Rounds 1–3 (5): Knit.

shape thumb gusset
Round 1: K14 (17), place a marker, increase in each of the next 2 stitches, place a marker, k to the end of the round—32 (38) stitches.
Round 2: Knit.
Round 3: K to marker, slip marker, increase in the next stitch, k to 1 stitch before the next marker, increase in the next stitch, slip marker, k to the end of the round—34 (40) stitches.
Round 4: Knit.
Rounds 5–6 (8): Repeat the last 2 rounds 1 (2) time(s)—36 (44) stitches, with 8 (10) stitches between the markers. Slip the stitches between the markers to a holder for the thumb.
Round 7 (9): Knit, casting on 2 stitches over the stitches on the holder—30 (36) stitches.
upper hand
Knit rounds until the piece measures 2 (3)" (5 [7.5]cm) above the thumb gusset.
shape top
Round 1: *K4, k2tog; repeat from * around—25 (30) stitches.
Round 2: Knit.
Round 3: *K3, k2tog; repeat from * around—20 (24) stitches.
Round 4: Knit.

Round 5: *K2, k2tog; repeat from * around—15 (18) stitches.

Round 6: Knit.

Round 7: *K1, k2tog; repeat from * around—10 (12) stitches.

Round 8: Knit.

Round 9: *K2tog; repeat from * around—5 (6) stitches.

Cut the yarn, leaving a long end. Use the yarn needle to thread the end through the remaining stitches. Draw together tightly and fasten off.

thumb

Slip the thumb stitches from the holder back to 1 larger double-pointed needle. Join the yarn and cast on 4 stitches—12 (14) stitches. Work back and forth on the 2 double-pointed needles in stockinette stitch (knit on right side, purl on wrong side) until the thumb measures 1½ (2)" (3.5 [5]cm) from the last row of the thumb gusset, ending with a wrong-side row.

Next row: K2tog across—6 (7) stitches. Cut the yarn, leaving a long end. Use the yarn needle to thread the end through the remaining stitches. Draw together tightly and fasten off.

FINISHING

Sew the thumb seam on the Medium and Large Mittens.

FRINGE

Cut twenty 5" (12.5cm) strands of yarn. Fold one strand in half and, with crochet hook, pull the folded end through the cuff edge of Mitten. Pull the ends through and tighten. Attach fringe evenly spaced around the cuff edge of each Mitten. Trim the fringe evenly. Weave in ends.

Whinny the Horse

(shown on page 51)

SIZES

3 years (4–5 years, 6–7 years)

FINISHED MEASUREMENTS

scarf: 5 x 21 (25, 29)" (12.5 x 53.5 [63.5, 74]cm)

hat circumference: 16 (18, 20)" (40.5 [45.5, 51]cm)

MATERIALS

- 1 skein each Brown Sheep Lamb's Pride Worsted, 85% wool, 15% mohair (4 oz [113.5g], 190 yd [173.5m]), #M175 Bronze Patina (A) and #M05 Onyx (B) **(4) medium**
- Size 7 (4.5mm) 16" (40cm) circular needle
- Size 7 (4.5mm) double-pointed needles, set of 5
- Size H-8 (5mm) crochet hook (for mane)

- Stitch markers
- 2 wiggle eyes, 1" (25mm) in diameter
- Craft glue
- Yarn needle

GAUGE

18 stitches and 25 rows = 4" (10cm) in stockinette stitch worked with a circular needle.

NOTE

The instructions are written for the smallest size, with changes for the larger sizes in parentheses. For ease in working, circle all numbers pertaining to your size.

HAT

Using the circular needle and A, cast on 72 (80, 88) stitches. Join, being careful not to twist the stitches. Place a marker for the beginning of the round. Work in stockinette stitch (knit every round) until the piece measures 4½ (5, 5½)" (11.5 [12.5, 14]cm) from the beginning.

shape crown

NOTE: Change to the double-pointed needles when the number of stitches has been sufficiently decreased.

Round 1: *K6, k2tog; repeat from * around—63 (70, 77) stitches.

Round 2: Knit.

Round 3: *K5, k2tog; repeat from * around—54 (60, 66) stitches.

Round 4: Knit.

Round 5: *K4, k2tog; repeat from * around—45 (50, 55) stitches.

Round 6: Knit.

Round 7: *K3, k2tog; repeat from * around—36 (40, 44) stitches.

Round 8: Knit.

Round 9: *K2, k2tog; repeat from * around—27 (30, 33) stitches.

Round 10: Knit.

Round 11: *K1, k2tog; repeat from * around—18 (20, 22) stitches.

Round 12: Knit.

Round 13: K2tog around—9 (10, 11) stitches.

Cut the yarn, leaving a long end. Use the yarn needle to thread the end through the remaining stitches. Draw together tightly and fasten off.

EAR (make 4)

NOTE: The ears are worked back and forth in rows on the circular needle.

Cast on 11 stitches.

Row 1: P2tog, p to the end of the row—10 stitches.

Row 2: K2tog, k to the end of the row—9 stitches.

Rows 3–10: Repeat the last 2 rows—1 stitch.

Bind off.

FINISHING

Place two ear pieces together with the right sides facing out and sew them together around the edges. Repeat for the other 2 ear pieces.

Sew the Ears to the top of the Hat.

Glue the eyes to the front of the Hat.

Using B, embroider 2 straight stitches below the eyes for the nostrils.

Weave in ends.

MANE

Cut forty 6" (15cm) lengths of B (or more, for a fuller look). Begin attaching the mane about 1½" (4cm) above the eyes and centered between the eyes, as follows: Fold a strand of yarn in half and, with crochet hook, pull the folded end through the Hat. Pull the ends through the loop formed by the folded end and tighten (as for fringe). Repeat this step all along the center line to about 3" (7.5cm) above the lower back edge. In the same way, attach 3 more rows of fringe, spaced close together. Trim the fringe ends evenly.

Weave in ends.

SCARF

NOTE: The Scarf is worked back and forth in rows on the circular needle.

Using the circular needle and A, cast on 23 stitches.

Rows 1–6: *K1, p1; repeat from * across, ending k1.

Row 7: (K1, p1) twice, k to last 4 stitches, (p1, k1) twice.

Row 8: (K1, p1) twice, k1, p to last 5 stitches, k1, (p1, k1) twice.

Repeat the last 2 rows until the piece measures 21 (25, 29)" (53.5 [63.5, 74]cm) from the beginning.

Last 6 rows: Repeat rows 1–6.

Bind off.

FRINGE

Cut twenty 10" (25.5cm) strands of B. Fold one strand in half and, with crochet hook, pull folded end through the end of the Scarf. Pull the ends through the loop formed by the folded end and tighten. Continue to attach fringe evenly spaced along both ends of the Scarf.

FINISHING

Trim the fringe ends evenly.

Weave in ends.

Truffles the Cat

(shown on page 52)

SIZES

3 years (4–5 years, 6–7 years)

FINISHED MEASUREMENTS

scarf: 5 x 21 (25, 29)" (12.5 x 53.5 [63.5, 74]cm)

hat circumference: 16 (18, 20)" (40.5 [45.5, 51]cm)

mitten length: 5½ (7, 9½)" (14 [18, 24]cm)

circumference: 5½ (6½, 8)" (14 [16.5, 20.5]cm)

MATERIALS

- 2 skeins Brown Sheep Lamb's Pride Worsted, 85% wool, 15% mohair (4 oz [113.5g], 190 yd [173.5m]), #M105 RPM Pink (A), and 1 skein #M05 Onyx (B) **4** medium
- Size 7 (4.5mm) 16" (40cm) circular needle
- Size 7 (4.5mm) double-pointed needles, set of 5
- Size 5 (3.75mm) double-pointed needles, set of 5
- Stitch markers

- Stitch holder (for Medium and Large mittens only)
- Small amount of polyester fiberfill stuffing
- 2 black buttons, ¼" (6mm) in diameter
- Yarn needle

GAUGE

18 stitches and 25 rows = 4" (10cm) in stockinette stitch worked with a circular needle.

NOTE

The instructions are written for the smallest size, with changes for the larger sizes in parentheses. For ease in working, circle all numbers pertaining to your size.

HAT

Using the circular needle and A, cast on 72 (80, 88) stitches. Join, being careful not to twist the stitches. Place a marker for the beginning of the round.
Work in stockinette stitch (knit every round) until the piece measures 4½ (5, 5½)" (11.5 [12.5, 14]cm) from the beginning.

shape crown

NOTE: Change to the larger double-pointed needles when the number of stitches has been sufficiently decreased.

Round 1: *K6, k2tog; repeat from * around—63 (70, 77) stitches.
Round 2: Knit.
Round 3: *K5, k2tog; repeat from * around—54 (60, 66) stitches.
Round 4: Knit.
Round 5: *K4, k2tog; repeat from * around—45 (50, 55) stitches.
Round 6: Knit.
Round 7: *K3, k2tog; repeat from * around—36 (40, 44) stitches.
Round 8: Knit.
Round 9: *K2, k2tog; repeat from * around—27 (30, 33) stitches.
Round 10: Knit.
Round 11: *K1, k2tog; repeat from * around—18 (20, 22) stitches.
Round 12: Knit.
Round 13: K2tog around—9 (10, 11) stitches.
Cut the yarn, leaving a long end. Use the yarn needle to thread the yarn end through the remaining stitches. Draw together tightly and fasten off.

EAR (make 4)

Using the larger double-pointed needles and B, cast on 11 stitches.
Row 1: Knit.
Row 2: P2tog, p to the end of the row—10 stitches.
Row 3: K2tog, k to the end of the row—9 stitches.
Rows 4–11: Repeat rows 2–3 four times—1 stitch.
Bind off.

FINISHING

Sew the Ears together in pairs and sew them to the top of the Hat.
Sew the buttons to the front of the Hat for eyes. Using B, embroider a straight-stitch nose below the eyes.
Cut 4 strands of B, each 6" (15cm) long. Using the yarn needle, weave the strands behind the nose, leaving the ends of the strands extending evenly on each side of the nose for whiskers. Trim the strands evenly.
Weave in ends.

SCARF

NOTE: The Scarf is worked back and forth in rows on a circular needle.

Using the circular needle and A, cast on 34 stitches.

Row 1: K1, p1 across.

Repeat row 1 until the piece measures 10½ (12½, 14½)" (26.5 [32, 37]cm).

Change to B and repeat row 1 until the piece measures 21 (25, 29)" (53.5 [63.5, 74]cm) from the beginning. Bind off.

FINISHING

Weave in ends.

MITTENS (make 2)

FOR SIZE SMALL ONLY

Using the smaller double-pointed needles and B, cast on 24 stitches. Divide the stitches evenly onto 4 needles. Join, being careful not to twist the stitches. Place a marker for the beginning of the round.

wrist ribbing

Work in k1, p1 rib for 1½" (3.8cm).

hand

Change to the larger double-pointed needles and A. Work in stockinette stitch until the piece measures 4½" (11.5cm) from the beginning.

shape top

Round 1: *K2, k2tog; repeat from * around—18 stitches.

Round 2: Knit.

Round 3: *K1, k2tog; repeat from * around—12 stitches.

Round 4: Knit.

Round 5: *K2tog; repeat from * around—6 stitches.

Round 6: Knit.

Round 7: *K2tog; repeat from * around—3 stitches.

Cut the yarn, leaving a long end. Use the yarn needle to thread the end through the remaining stitches. Draw together tightly and fasten off.

FOR SIZES MEDIUM (LARGE)

Using the smaller double-pointed needles and B, cast on 30 (36) stitches. Divide the stitches evenly onto 4 needles. Join, being careful not to twist the stitches. Place a marker for the beginning of the round.

wrist ribbing

Work in k1, p1 rib for 2 (3)" (5 [7.5]cm).

lower hand

Change to the larger double-pointed needles and A.

Rounds 1–3 (5): Knit.

shape thumb gusset

Round 1: K14 (17), place a marker, increase in each of the next 2 stitches, place a marker, k to the end of the round—32 (38) stitches.

Round 2: Knit.

Round 3: K to the next marker, slip marker, increase in the next stitch, k to 1 stitch before the next marker, increase in the next stitch, slip marker, k to the end of the round—34 (40) stitches.

Round 4: Knit.

Rounds 5–6 (8): Repeat the last 2 rounds 1 (2) time(s)—36 (44) stitches, with 8 (10) stitches between the markers. Slip the stitches between the markers to a holder for the thumb.

Round 7 (9): Knit, casting on 2 stitches over the stitches on the holder—30 (36) stitches.

upper hand

Knit rounds until the piece measures 2 (3)" (5 [7.5]cm) above the thumb gusset.

shape top

Round 1: *K4, k2tog; repeat from * around—25 (30) stitches.

Round 2: Knit.

Round 3: *K3, k2tog; repeat from * around—20 (24) stitches.

Round 4: Knit.

Round 5: *K2, k2tog; repeat from * around—15 (18) stitches.

Round 6: Knit.

Round 7: *K1, k2tog; repeat from * around—10 (12) stitches.

Round 8: Knit.

Round 9: *K2tog around—5 (6) stitches.

Cut the yarn, leaving a long end. Use the yarn needle to thread the end through the remaining stitches. Draw together tightly and fasten off.

thumb

Slip the thumb stitches from the holder back to one of the larger double-pointed needles. Join the yarn and cast on 4 stitches—12 (14) stitches.

Work back and forth on 2 double-pointed needles in stockinette stitch (knit on the right side, purl on the wrong side) until the thumb measures 1½ (2)" (3.5 [5]cm) from the last row of the thumb gusset, ending with a wrong-side row.

Next row: K2tog across—6 (7) stitches. Cut the yarn, leaving a long end. Use the yarn needle to thread the end through the remaining stitches. Draw together tightly and fasten off.

EAR (make 4)

Using the larger double-pointed needles and B, cast on 6 stitches.

Row 1: Knit.

Row 2: Purl.

Row 3: K2tog, k to the last 2 stitches, k2tog—4 stitches.

Row 4: Purl.

Row 5: K2tog twice—2 stitches.

Row 6: Purl.

Row 7: K2tog—1 stitch.

Bind off.

FINISHING

Sew the thumb seam on the Medium and Large Mittens.

Sew the Ears together in pairs and sew 2 Ears to one side of each Mitten, slightly below the thumb placement.

Using B, embroider straight-stitch eyes below the Ears on each Mitten.

Using B, embroider a back-stitch mouth and nose under the eyes on each Mitten.

Using B, embroider 3 whiskers, each 1" (2.5cm) long, on each side of the nose.

Weave in ends.

03　Intermediate

Ling-Ling the Panda Bear

Faux fur yarn makes this sweet set as soft as a baby panda. The hat is knit flat and seamed, and the ears are knit in the round and stuffed with leftover yarn. The eyes are added by the intarsia method. Don't worry if you haven't done it before—just follow the Instructions and have fun!

Instructions on page 78.

Wag the Dog

Knit this sweet doggie hat flat and seam it when you're done.
A little bit of intarsia for the eyes adds a lot of interest to the knitting.
For the nose, use a store-bought pom-pom or make your own!

Instructions on page 81.

Ringo the Dog

Easy embellishment takes this hat from simple to doggone cute! The puppy's ears are knit in the round—slipped stitches at the sides make the ears lie flat.

Instructions on page 85.

Wanda the Fish

You won't be fishing for compliments when your little one goes out in this hat! Tropical colors and warm, woolly yarn come together in a playful topper. The fins and mouth are knit separately and sewn on.

Instructions on page 86.

Scottie the Dog

A parade of Scottie dogs encircles this stocking hat. Knit-in motifs accent the hat and ends of the scarf. Easy duplicate stitch dogs on mittens completes the set.

nstructions on page 88.

Ling-Ling the Panda Bear

(shown on page 73)

SIZES

3 years (4–5 years, 6–7 years)

FINISHED MEASUREMENTS

scarf: 5 x 21 (25, 29)" (12.5 x 53.5 [63.5, 74]cm)

hat circumference: 16 (18, 20)" (40.5 [45.5, 51]cm)

mitten length: 5½ (7, 9½)" (14 [18, 24]cm)

circumference: 5½ (6½, 8)" (14 [16.5, 20.5]cm)

MATERIALS

- 3 skeins Reynolds Frisky, 60% cotton, 40% nylon (1¾ oz [50g], 81 yd [74m]), #1 White (A), and 2 skeins #18 Black (B)

  4 medium
- Size 7 (4.5mm) needles
- Size 7 (4.5mm) double-pointed needles, set of 5
- Size 5 (3.75mm) double-pointed needles, set of 5
- Stitch markers
- Stitch holder (for Medium and Large mittens only)
- 2 wiggle eyes, ½" (13mm) in diameter
- Craft glue
- Yarn needle

GAUGE

18 stitches and 25 rows = 4" (10cm) in stockinette stitch with a circular needle.

NOTE

The instructions are written for the smallest size, with changes for the larger sizes in parentheses. For ease in working, circle all numbers pertaining to your size.

HAT

NOTE: Work the eyes using the chart or by following the row instructions. Use a separate ball of yarn for each color; do not carry the unused color on the wrong side of work.

Using the straight needles and A, cast on 72 (80, 88) stitches. Work in stockinette stitch (knit on the right side, purl on the wrong side) until the piece measures 2 (2½, 2½)" (5 [6.5, 6.5]cm from the beginning), ending with a wrong-side row.

work eyes (see chart)

Row 1: With A k24 (28, 32), with B k4, with A k16, with B k4, with A k to the end of the row.

Row 2: With A p23 (27, 31), with B p6, with A p14, with B p6, with A p to the end of the row.

Row 3: With A k22 (26, 30), with B k8, with A k12, with B k8, with A k to the end of the row.

Row 4: With A p22 (26, 30), with B p9, with A p10, with B p9, with A p to the end of the row.

Row 5: With A k22 (26, 30), with B k11, with A k6, with B k11, with A k to the end of the row.

Row 6: With A p22 (26, 30), with B p11,

with A p6, with B p11, with A p to the end of the row.

Row 7: With A k22 (26, 30), with B k11, with A k6, with B k11, with A k to the end of the row.

Row 8: With A p22 (26, 30), with B p11, with A p6, with B p11, with A p to the end of the row.

Row 9: With A k23 (27, 31), with B k10, with A k6, with B k10, with A k to the end of the row.

Row 10: With A p24 (28, 32), with B p9, with A p6, with B p9, with A p to the end of the row.

Row 11: With A k25 (29, 33), with B k7, with A k8, with B k7, with A k to the end of the row.

Row 12: With A p26 (30, 34), with B p5, with A p10, with B p5, with A p to the end of the row.

Row 13: With A k27 (31, 35), with B k4, with A k10, with B k4, with A k to the end of the row. Fasten off B, and continue with A only until the piece measures 4½ (5, 5½)" (11.5 [12.5, 14]cm) from the beginning, ending with a wrong-side row.

shape crown

Row 1: *K6, k2tog; repeat from * around—63 (70, 77) stitches.

Even-Numbered Rows 2–12: Purl.

Row 3: *K5, k2tog; repeat from * around—54 (60, 66) stitches.

Row 5: *K4, k2tog; repeat from * around—45 (50, 55) stitches.

Row 7: *K3, k2tog; repeat from * around—36 (40, 44) stitches.

Row 9: *K2, k2tog; repeat from * around—27 (30, 33) stitches.

Row 11: *K1, k2tog; repeat from * around—18 (20, 22) stitches.

Row 13: K2tog around—9 (10, 11) stitches. Cut the yarn, leaving a long end. Use the yarn needle to thread the end through the remaining stitches. Draw together tightly. Sew the back seam and fasten off.

EAR (make 2)

Using the larger double-pointed needles and B, cast on 20 stitches. Divide the stitches onto 4 needles—5 stitches per needle. Join, being careful not to twist the stitches. Place a marker for the beginning of the round.

Rounds 1–4: Knit.

Round 5: On the first needle, k2tog, k to the end of the needle; on the second needle, k to the last 2 stitches, k2tog; on the third needle, k2tog, k to the end of needle; on the fourth needle, k to the last 2 stitches, k2tog—4 stitches on each needle.

Rounds 6–7: Repeat round 5 twice—2 stitches remain on each needle. Slip the stitches from the first and second needles onto the first needle; slip stitches from the third and fourth needles onto the third needle. Cut the yarn, leaving a long end. Hold the first and third needles parallel to each other and use the end to graft the stitches together.

FINISHING

Stuff each Ear with about 12" (30.5cm) of matching yarn.

Sew the Ears to the top of the Hat. Glue the eyes to the front of the Hat. With B, embroider a triangle shape with straight stitches for the nose. Weave in ends.

SCARF

Using the straight needles and A, cast on 23 stitches.

Row 1: *K1, p1; repeat from * across. Repeat the last row until the piece measures 10½ (12½, 14½)" (26.5 [32, 37]cm) from the beginning.

Change to B and continue in the pattern as established until the piece measures 21 (25, 29)" (53.5 [63.5, 74]cm) from the beginning. Bind off.

FINISHING
Weave in ends.

MITTENS (make 2)
FOR SIZE SMALL ONLY
Using the smaller double-pointed needles and B, cast on 24 stitches. Divide the stitches evenly onto 4 needles. Join, being careful not to twist the stitches. Place a marker for the beginning of the round.

wrist ribbing
Work in k1, p1 rib for 1½" (3.8cm).

hand
Change to the larger double-pointed needles and A. Work in stockinette stitch (knit every round) until the piece measures 4½" (11.5cm).

shape top
Round 1: *K2, k2tog; repeat from * around—18 stitches.
Round 2: Knit.
Round 3: *K1, k2tog; repeat from * around—12 stitches.
Round 4: Knit.
Round 5: *K2tog; repeat from * around—6 stitches.
Round 6: Knit.
Round 7: *K2tog; repeat from * around—3 stitches.
Cut the yarn, leaving a long end. Use the yarn needle to thread the end through the remaining stitches. Draw together tightly and fasten off.

FOR SIZES MEDIUM (LARGE)
Using the smaller double-pointed needles and B, cast on 30 (36) stitches. Divide the stitches evenly onto 4 needles. Join, being careful not to twist the stitches. Place a marker for the beginning of the round.

wrist ribbing
Work in k1, p1 rib for 2 (3)" (5 [7.5]cm).

lower hand
Change to the larger double-pointed needles and A.
Rounds 1–3 (5): Knit.

shape thumb gusset
Round 1: K14 (17), place a marker, increase in each of the next 2 stitches, place a marker, k to the end of the round—32 (38) stitches.
Round 2: Knit.
Round 3: K to the next marker, slip marker, increase in the next stitch, k to 1 stitch before the next marker, increase in the next stitch, slip marker, k to the end of the round—34 (40) stitches.
Round 4: Knit.
Rounds 5–6 (8): Repeat the last 2 rounds 1 (2) times—36 (44) stitches, with 8 (10) stitches between the markers. Slip the stitches between the markers to a holder for the thumb.
Round 7 (9): Knit, casting on 2 stitches over the stitches on the holder—30 (36) stitches.

upper hand
Knit until the piece measures 2 (3)" (5 [7.5]cm) above the thumb gusset.

shape top
Round 1: *K4, k2tog; repeat from * around—25 (30) stitches.
Round 2: Knit.
Round 3: *K3, k2tog; repeat from * around—20 (24) stitches.
Round 4: Knit.
Round 5: *K2, k2tog; repeat from * around—15 (18) stitches.
Round 6: Knit.
Round 7: *K1, k2tog; repeat from * around—10 (12) stitches.

Round 8: Knit.

Round 9: *K2tog; repeat from * around—5 (6) stitches.

Cut the yarn, leaving a long end. Use the yarn needle to thread the end through the remaining stitches. Draw together tightly and fasten off.

thumb

Slip the thumb stitches from the holder back to 1 larger double-pointed needle. Join the yarn and cast on 4 stitches—12 (14) stitches. Work back and forth on 2 double-pointed needles in stockinette stitch (knit on right side, purl on wrong side) until the thumb measures 1½ (2)" (3.5 [5]cm) from the last row of the thumb gusset, ending with a wrong-side row.

Next row: K2tog across—6 (7) stitches. Cut the yarn, leaving a long end. Use the yarn needle to thread the end through the remaining stitches. Draw together tightly and fasten off.

FINISHING

Sew the thumb seam on Medium and Large Mittens.

Weave in ends.

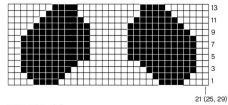

13
11
9
7
5
3
1

21 (25, 29)

☐ #1 White (A)
■ #18 Black (B)

Wag the Dog

(shown on page 74)

SIZES

3 years (4–5 years, 6–7 years)

FINISHED MEASUREMENTS

scarf: 5 x 21 (25, 29)" (12.5 x 53.5 [63.5, 74]cm)
hat circumference: 16 (18, 20)" (40.5 [45.5, 51]cm)
mitten length: 5½ (7, 9½)" (14 [18, 24]cm)
circumference: 5½ (6½, 8)" (14 [16.5, 20.5]cm)

MATERIALS

• 2 skeins Brown Sheep Lamb's Pride Worsted, 85% wool, 15% mohair (4 oz [113.5], 190 yd [173.5m]), #M10 Créme (A),

and 1 skein #M164 Brown Bear (B) **4** **medium**

• Size 7 (4.5mm) needles
• Size 7 (4.5mm) double-pointed needles, set of 5
• Size 5 (3.75mm) double-pointed needles, set of 5
• Stitch markers
• Stitch holder (for Medium and Large mittens only)
• 2 wiggle eyes, 1" (25mm) in diameter
• Craft glue
• 1 black pom-pom, 1" (25mm) in diameter
• Yarn needle

INTERMEDIATE

GAUGE

18 stitches and 25 rows = 4" (10cm) in stockinette stitch with larger needles.

NOTE

The instructions are written for the smallest size, with changes for the larger sizes in parentheses. For ease in working, circle all numbers pertaining to your size.

HAT

NOTE: Work the eye from the chart or by following the row instructions. Use a separate ball of yarn for each color; do not carry the unused color on the wrong side of work.

Using the straight needles and A, cast on 72 (80, 88) stitches. Work in stockinette stitch (knit on right side, purl on wrong side) until the piece measures 2 (2½, 2½)" (5 [6.5, 6.5]cm) from the beginning, ending with a right-side row.

work eye (see chart)

Row 1 (wrong side): With A p43 (47, 51), with B p4, with A p to the end of the row.

Row 2: With A k24 (28, 32), with B k6, with A k to the end of the row.

Row 3: With A p41 (45, 49), with B p8, with A p to the end of the row.

Row 4: With A k22 (26, 30), with B k10, with A k to the end of the row.

Row 5: With A p40 (44, 48), with B p10, with A p to the end of the row.

Row 6: With A k21 (25, 29), with B k12, with A k to the end of the row.

Row 7: With A p39 (43, 47), with B p12, with A p to the end of the row.

Row 8: With A k21 (25, 29), with B k12, with A k to the end of the row.

Rows 9–10: Repeat rows 7–8.

Row 11: With A p40 (44, 48), with B p10, with A p to the end of the row.

Row 12: With A k22 (26, 30), with B k10, with A k to the end of the row.

Row 13: With A p41 (45, 49), with B p8, with A p to the end of the row.

Row 14: With A k24 (28, 32), with B k6, with A k to the end of the row.

Row 15: With A p43 (47, 51), with B p4, with A p to the end of the row.

End off B, and continue with A only until the piece measures 4½ (5, 5½)" (11.5 [12.5, 14]cm) from the beginning, ending with a wrong-side row.

shape crown

Row 1: *K6, k2tog; repeat from * around—63 (70, 77) stitches.

Row 2: Purl.

Row 3: *K5, k2tog; repeat from * around—54 (60, 66) stitches.

Row 4: Purl.

Row 5: *K4, k2tog; repeat from * around—45 (50, 55) stitches.

Row 6: Purl.

Row 7: *K3, k2tog; repeat from * around—36 (40, 44) stitches.

Row 8: Purl.

Row 9: *K2, k2tog; repeat from * around—27 (30, 33) stitches.

Row 10: Purl.

Row 11: *K1, k2tog; repeat from * around—18 (20, 22) stitches.

Row 12: Purl.

Row 13: K2tog around—9 (10, 11) stitches.

Cut the yarn, leaving a long end. Use the yarn needle to thread the end through the remaining stitches. Draw together tightly. Sew the back seam and fasten off.

EAR (make 2; 1 with A and 1 with B)

Using the larger double-pointed needles, cast on 24 stitches. Divide the stitches evenly onto 4 needles—6 stitches per needle. Join, being careful not to twist the stitches. Place a marker for the beginning of the round. Work in stockinette stitch (knit every round) until the piece measures 3" (7.5cm) from the beginning.

shape ear

Round 1: K2tog, k1, ssk, k7, k2tog, k1, ssk, k7—20 stitches.
Round 2: Knit.
Round 3: K2tog, k1, ssk, k5, k2tog, k1, ssk, k5—16 stitches.
Round 4: Knit.
Round 5: K2tog, k1, ssk, k3, k2tog, k1, ssk, k3—12 stitches.
Round 6: Knit.
Round 7: K2tog, k1, ssk, k1, k2tog, k1, ssk, k1—8 stitches.
Round 8: Knit.

Cut the yarn, leaving a long end. Use the yarn needle to thread the end through the remaining stitches. Draw together tightly and fasten off.

FINISHING

Sew the cast-on edge of the Ears to the top of the Hat.
Fold the tops of the Ears down and sew them in place.
Glue the eyes to the front of the Hat.
Sew the pom-pom to the front of the Hat for the nose.
Weave in ends.

MITTENS FOR SIZE SMALL ONLY

Using the smaller double-pointed needles and A, cast on 24 stitches. Divide the stitches evenly onto 4 needles; 6 stitches per needle. Join, while being careful not to twist the stitches. Place a marker for the beginning of the round.

wrist ribbing

Work in k1, p1 rib for 1 1/2" (3.8cm).

hand

Change to the larger double-pointed needles and work in stockinette stitch until the piece measures 4 1/2" (11.5cm) from the beginning.

shape top

Round 1: *K2, k2tog; repeat from * around—18 stitches.
Round 2: Knit.
Round 3: *K1, k2tog; repeat from * around—12 stitches.
Round 4: Knit.
Round 5: *K2tog; repeat from * around—6 stitches.
Round 6: Knit.
Round 7: *K2tog; repeat from * around—3 stitches.

Cut the yarn, leaving a long end. Pull the end through the remaining stitches, draw together tightly, and fasten off.

FOR SIZES MEDIUM (LARGE)

Using the smaller double-pointed needles and A, cast on 30 (36) stitches. Divide the stitches evenly onto 4 needles. Join, while being careful not to twist the stitches. Place a marker for the beginning of the round.

wrist ribbing

Work in k1, p1 rib for 2 (3)" (5 [7.5]cm).

lower hand

Change to the larger double-pointed needles.
Rounds 1–3 (5): Knit.

shape thumb gusset

Round 1: K14 (17), place a marker, increasing in each of the next 2 stitches, place a marker, k to the end of the round—32 (38) stitches.
Round 2: Knit.
Round 3: K to marker, slip marker,

increasing in the next stitch, k to 1 stitch before the next marker, increasing in the next stitch, slip marker, k to the end of the round—34 (40) stitches.

Round 4: Knit.

Rounds 5–6 (8): Repeat last 2 rounds 1 (2) times—36 (44) stitches, with 8 (10) stitches between the markers. Slip the stitches between the markers to a holder for the thumb.

Round 7 (9): Knit, casting on 2 stitches over the stitches on the holder—30 (36) stitches.

upper hand

Knit rounds until the piece measures 2 (3)" (5 [7.5]cm) above the thumb gusset.

shape top

Round 1: *K4, k2tog; repeat from * around—25 (30) stitches.

Round 2: Knit.

Round 3: *K3, k2tog; repeat from * around—20 (24) stitches.

Round 4: Knit.

Round 5: *K2, k2tog; repeat from * around—15 (18) stitches.

Round 6: Knit.

Round 7: *K1, k2tog; repeat from * around—10 (12) stitches.

Round 8: Knit.

Round 9: *K2tog; repeat from * around—5 (6) stitches.

Cut the yarn, leaving a long end for sewing. Pull the end through the remaining stitches, draw together tightly, and fasten off.

thumb

Slip the thumb stitches from the holder back to 1 larger double-pointed needle. Join the yarn and cast on 4 stitches—12 (14) stitches. Work back and forth on 2 double-pointed needles in stockinette stitch (knit on right side, purl on wrong side) until the thumb measures 1 1/2 (2)" (3.5 [5]cm) from the last row of the thumb gusset, ending with a wrong-side row.

Next row: K2tog across—6 (7) stitches.

Cut the yarn, leaving a long end for sewing. Pull the end through the remaining stitches, draw together tightly, and fasten off.

EAR (make 4)

Using the larger double-pointed needles and A, cast on 16 stitches. Divide the stitches evenly onto 4 needles—4 stitches per needle. Join, while being careful not to twist the stitches. Place a marker for the beginning of the round.

Rounds 1–3: Knit.

Round 4: K2tog, k1, ssk, k3, k2tog, k1, ssk, k3—12 stitches.

Round 5: Knit.

Round 6: K2tog, k1, ssk, k1, k2tog, k1, ssk, k1—8 stitches.

Cut the yarn, leaving a long end for sewing. Divide the remaining stitches onto 2 needles, 4 stitches per needle, and use the end to graft the stitches together.

FINISHING

Sew the thumb seam on Medium and Large Mittens.

Using B, embroider a chain stitch over one side of each ear, leaving a 1-stitch (or 1-row) border of A.

Sew the cast-on edges of the 2 ears to the tips, and off to the side, of each Mitten.

Weave in ends.

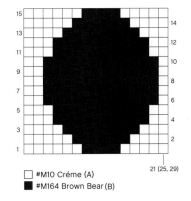

□ #M10 Créme (A)
■ #M164 Brown Bear (B)

21 (25, 29)

Ringo the Dog

(shown on page 75)

SIZES

3 years (4–5 years, 6–7 years)

FINISHED MEASUREMENTS

hat circumference: 16 (18, 20)" (40.5 [45.5, 51]cm)

MATERIALS

- 1 skein each Brown Sheep Lamb's Pride Worsted, 85% wool, 15% mohair (4 oz [113.5g], 190 yd [173.5m]), #M07 Sable (A) and #M05 Onyx (B) (4) **medium**
- Size 7 (4.5mm) 16" (40cm) circular needle
- Size 7 (4.5mm) double-pointed needles, set of 5
- Stitch markers
- Yarn needle
- 2 brown animal (crystal) eyes, ½" (13mm) in diameter
- Craft glue
- 1 black pom-pom, 1" (25mm) in diameter

GAUGE

18 stitches and 25 rows = 4" (10cm) in stockinette stitch with a circular needle.

HAT

Using the circular needle and A, cast on 72 (80, 88) stitches. Join, being careful not to twist the stitches. Place a marker for the beginning of the round.

Work in stockinette stitch (knit every round) until the piece measures 4½ (5, 5½)" (11.5 [12.5, 14]cm) from the beginning.

shape crown

NOTE: Change to the larger double-pointed needles when the number of stitches has been sufficiently decreased.

Round 1: *K6, k2tog; repeat from * around—(70, 77) stitches.

Round 2: Knit.

Round 3: *K5, k2tog; repeat from * around—54 (60, 66) stitches.

Round 4: Knit.

Round 5: *K4, k2tog; repeat from * around—45 (50, 55) stitches.

Round 6: Knit.

Round 7: *K3, k2tog; repeat from * around—36 (40, 44) stitches.

Round 8: Knit.

Round 9: *K2, k2tog; repeat from * around—27 (30, 33) stitches.

Round 10: Knit.

Round 11: *K1, k2tog; repeat from * around—18 (20, 22) stitches.

Round 12: Knit.

Round 13: K2tog around—9 (10, 11) stitches.

Cut the yarn, leaving a long end. Use the yarn needle to thread the end through the remaining stitches. Draw together tightly and fasten off.

EAR (make 2)

Using the double-pointed needles and B, cast on 14 stitches. Divide the stitches as evenly as possible onto 4 needles. Join, being careful not to twist the stitches. Place a marker for the beginning of the round.

shape ear

Round 1: Knit.

Round 2: K6, slip the next stitch, k6, slip the last stitch.

Repeat the last 2 rounds until the piece measures 4½" (11.5cm) from the beginning.

Next round: K2tog, k2, k2tog, slip the next stitch, k2tog, k2, k2tog, slip the last stitch.

Next round: Knit.

Next round: (K2tog) twice, slip the next stitch, (k2tog) twice, slip the last stitch. Bind off.

Flatten the ear with slipped stitches at the sides. Sew the bound-off edge together.

FINISHING

Sew ears to the top of the Hat. Snap off the shank on the back of the eyes. Glue the eyes to the front of the Hat. Sew pom-pom to the front of the Hat for the nose. Weave in ends.

Wanda the Fish

(shown on page 76)

SIZES

3 years (4–5 years, 6–7 years)

FINISHED MEASUREMENTS

hat circumference: 16 (18, 20)" (40.5 [45.5, 51]cm)

MATERIALS

- 1 skein each Brown Sheep Lamb's Pride Worsted, 85% wool, 15% mohair (4 oz [113.5g], 190 yd [173.5m]), #M78 Aztec Turquoise (A), #M120 Limeade (B), #M155 Lemon Drop (C), and #M83 Raspberry (D) 4 **medium**
- Size 7 (4.5mm) 16" (40cm) circular needle
- Size 7 (4.5mm) double-pointed needles, set of 5
- Stitch markers
- Yarn needle
- 2 wiggle eyes, ¼" (6mm) in diameter
- Craft glue

GAUGE

18 stitches and 25 rows = 4" (10cm) in stockinette stitch worked with a circular needle.

NOTE

The instructions are written for the smallest size, with the changes for the larger sizes in parentheses.

For ease in working, circle all numbers pertaining to your size.

HAT

Using the circular needle and A, cast on 72 (80, 88) stitches. Join, being careful not to twist the stitches. Place a marker for the beginning of the round. Work in stockinette stitch (knit every round) until the piece measures 4½ (5, 5½)" (11.5 [12.5, 14]cm) from the beginning.

shape crown

NOTE: Change to the larger double-pointed needles when the number of stitches has been sufficiently decreased.

Round 1: *K6, k2tog; repeat from * around—63 (70, 77) stitches.

Round 2: Knit.

Round 3: *K5, k2tog; repeat from * around—54 (60, 66) stitches.

Round 4: Knit.

Round 5: *K4, k2tog; repeat from * around—45 (50, 55) stitches.

Round 6: Knit.

Round 7: *K3, k2tog; repeat from * around—36 (40, 44) stitches.

Round 8: Knit.

Round 9: *K2, k2tog; repeat from * around—27 (30, 33) stitches.

Round 10: Knit.

Round 11: *K1, k2tog; repeat from * around—18 (20, 22) stitches.

Round 12: Knit.

Round 13: K2tog around—9 (10, 11) stitches.

Cut the yarn, leaving a long end. Use the yarn needle to thread the end through the remaining stitches. Draw together tightly and fasten off.

FINISHING

Glue the eyes to the front of the Hat.

FIN (make 4)

Using 2 double-pointed needles and B, cast on 5 stitches.

Row 1: Knit.

Row 2: Increase 1 stitch in the first stitch, p to the end of the row—6 stitches.

Row 3: Increase 1 stitch in the first stitch, k to the end of the row—7 stitches.

Rows 4–11: Repeat rows 2–3 four times—15 stitches. Bind off.

Sew the fin pieces together in pairs, the increased side edges and along the bound-off edge. Sew a Fin to each side of the Hat, with the top edge below the row on which the eyes are attached.

TOP FIN

Using the double-pointed needles and C, cast on 7 stitches.

Rows 1–11: Work rows 1–11 of Fin—17 stitches. Bind off.

Fold the Top Fin in half, matching the increased side edges. Sew seam along the bound-off and side edge. Sew the Top Fin to center top of the Hat.

MOUTH

Using the double-pointed needles and D, cast on 13 stitches. Join, being careful not to twist stitches. Place a marker for the beginning of the round.

Rounds 1–5: Knit. Bind off. Sew the cast-on edge to the Hat.

Weave in ends.

Scottie the Dog

(shown on page 77)

SIZES

3 years (4–5 years, 6–7 years)

FINISHED MEASUREMENTS

hat circumference: 16 (18, 20)" (40.5 [45.5, 51]cm)

scarf: 6 x 30 (40)" (15 x 76 [101.5]cm)

mitten length: 5½ (7, 9½)" (14 [18, 24]cm)

circumference: 5½ (6½, 8)" (14 [16.5, 20.5]cm)

MATERIALS

• 6 balls Lion Brand Lion Cashmere Blend, 72% merino
wool, 15% nylon, 13% cashmere [1½ oz [40g], 84 yd [77m]),
#150 Silver (A) **(4)** **medium**

• 1 ball Lion Brand Tiffany, 100% nylon ([1¾ oz [50g], 137 yd
[125m]), #153 Black (B)

• Size 7 (4.5mm) needles

• Size 5 (3.75mm) needles

• Size 7 (4.5mm) double-pointed needles, set of 5

• Size 5 (3.75mm) double-pointed needles, set of 5

• Stitch markers

• Stitch holder (for Medium and Large Mittens only)

• Small amount of red worsted-weight yarn for dog collars
and tassel

• 3" (7.5cm) piece of heavy cardboard

• Yarn needle

GAUGE

18 stitches and 25 rows = 4" (10cm) in stockinette stitch with
larger needles.

NOTE

Instructions are written for the smallest size, with changes
for the larger sizes in parentheses. For ease in working,
circle all numbers pertaining to your size.

HAT

Using the smaller straight needles
and A, cast on 68 (76, 88) stitches.

Rows 1–3: Using A, knit.

Row 4: Knit, increasing 4 stitches
evenly spaced across the row—72
(80, 92) stitches.

Change to the larger straight needles.

Rows 5, 7 and 9: Purl.

Rows 6 and 8: Knit.

work Scottie Dog motifs (see chart)

Row 1 (right side): K2 (3, 4), work row
1 of Scottie Dog chart, *k3 (5, 8), work
row 1 of Scottie Dog chart; repeat from
* twice more; k1 (2, 4).

Row 2: P1 (2, 4), work row 2 of Scottie Dog chart, *p3 (5, 8), work row 2 of
Scottie Dog chart; repeat from * twice
more; p2 (3, 4).

Row 3: K2 (3, 4), work row 3 of Scottie
Dog chart, *k3 (5, 8), work row 3 of
Scottie Dog chart; repeat from * twice
more; k1 (2, 4).

Rows 4–15: Repeat rows 2–3 six times, working consecutive rows of Scottie Dog chart.

Row 16: Purl.

shaping

Row 1 (right side decrease row): K16 (18, 21), place a marker, k2togb, k2tog, k32 (36, 42), k2togb, k2tog, place a marker, k16 (18, 21)—68 (76, 88) stitches.

Row 2: Purl.

Row 3: Knit

Row 4: Purl.

Row 5 (decrease row): K to 1 stitch before the first marker, k2togb, k2tog, k to 3 stitches before the next marker, k2togb, k2tog, k to the end—64 (72, 84) stitches.

Repeat rows 2–5 until 12 stitches remain.

Cut the yarn, leaving a long end. Use the yarn needle to thread the end through the remaining stitches. Draw together tightly. Sew the back seam and fasten off.

TASSEL (make 1)

Cut two 5" (12.5cm) lengths of red worsted-weight yarn and set aside.

Wrap the red worsted-weight yarn around the cardboard about 20 times. With one 5" (12.5cm) length of yarn, tie strands together at one edge of the cardboard. Cut strands at the opposite edge of the cardboard. Tie the other 5" (13cm) length around the Tassel, about 1" (2.5cm) below the top tie for the Tassel neck. Thread the ends of the neck tie through the Tassel. Trim the ends of the Tassel evenly. Thread the ends of the top tie through the end of the Hat and knot on the wrong side to secure.

FINISHING

Using the red worsted-weight yarn, embroider a straight-stitch collar on each dog. Weave in ends.

SCARF

Using the larger straight needles and A, cast on 27 stitches.

Rows 1–4 (seed stitch): *K1, p1; repeat from * across to last stitch, k1.

Row 5: (K1, p1) twice, k to the last 4 stitches, (p1, k1) twice.

Row 6: (K1, p1) twice, p to the last 4 stitches, (p1, k1) twice.

Rows 7–8: Repeat rows 5–6.

work Scottie Dog motif (see chart)

Row 9 (right side): (K1, p1) twice, k2, work row 1 of Scottie Dog chart, k2, (p1, k1) twice.

Row 10: (K1, p1) twice, p2, work row 2 of Scottie Dog chart, p2, (p1, k1) twice.

Row 11: (K1, p1) twice, k2, work row 3 of Scottie Dog chart, k2, (p1, k1) twice.

Rows 12–23: Repeat rows 10–11 six times, working consecutive rows of Scottie Dog chart.

Row 24 (wrong side): (K1, p1) twice, p to the last 4 stitches, (p1, k1) twice.

Row 25: (K1, p1) twice, k to the last 4 stitches (p1, k1) twice.

Repeat rows 24–25 until the piece measures 26 (36)" (66 [91.5]cm) from the beginning, ending with a wrong-side row.

work Scottie Dog motif (see chart)

NOTE: To work the Scottie Dog facing in the opposite direction, read right-side rows of the chart from left to right and wrong-side rows from right to left.

Row 1 (right side): (K1, p1) twice, k2, work row 15 of Scottie Dog chart, k2, (p1, k1) twice.

Row 2: (K1, p1) twice, p2, work row 14 of Scottie Dog chart, p2, (p1, k1) twice.

Row 3: (K1, p1) twice, k2, work row 13 of Scottie Dog chart, k2, (p1, k1) twice.

Rows 4–15: Repeat rows 2–3 six times, working consecutive rows of Scottie Dog chart.

Row 16: (K1, p1) twice, p to the last 4 stitches, (p1, k1) twice.

Row 17: (K1, p1) twice, k to the last 4 stitches, (p1, k1) twice.

Rows 18–19: Repeat rows 16–17.

Rows 20–23: *K1, p1; repeat from * across to the last stitch, k1.

Bind off.

FINISHING

Using the red worsted-weight yarn, embroider a straight-stitch collar on the neck of each Scottie Dog motif. Weave in ends.

MITTENS (make 2)

FOR SIZE SMALL ONLY

Using the smaller double-pointed needles and A, cast on 24 stitches. Divide the stitches evenly onto 4 needles—6 stitches per needle. Join, being careful not to twist the stitches.

Place a marker for the beginning of the round.

wrist ribbing

Work in k1, p1 rib for 1½" (3.8cm).

hand

Change to the larger double-pointed needles and work in stockinette stitch until the piece measures 4½" (11.5cm) from the beginning.

shape top

Round 1: *K2, k2tog; repeat from * around—18 stitches.

Round 2: Knit.

Round 3: *K1, k2tog; repeat from * around—12 stitches.

Round 4: Knit.

Round 5: *K2tog; repeat from * around—6 stitches.

Round 6: Knit.

Round 7: *K2tog; repeat from * around—3 stitches.

Cut the yarn, leaving a long end. Pull the end through the remaining stitches, draw together tightly, and fasten off.

FOR SIZES MEDIUM (LARGE)

Using the smaller double-pointed needles and A, cast on 30 (36) stitches. Divide the stitches evenly

onto 4 needles. Join, being careful not to twist the stitches. Place a marker for the beginning of the round.

wrist ribbing

Work in k1, p1 rib for 2 (3)" (5 [7.5]cm).

lower hand

Change to the larger double-pointed needles.

Rounds 1–3 (5): Knit.

shape thumb gusset

Round 1: K14 (17), place a marker, increase in each of the next 2 stitches, place a marker, k to the end of the round—32 (38) stitches.

Round 2: Knit.

Round 3: K to marker, slip marker, increase in the next stitch, k to 1 stitch before the next marker, increase in the next stitch, slip marker, k to the end of the round—34 (40) stitches.

Round 4: Knit.

Rounds 5–6 (8): Repeat the last 2 rounds 1 (2) time(s)—36 (44) stitches, with 8 (10) stitches between markers. Slip the stitches between the markers to a holder for the thumb.

Round 7 (9): Knit, casting on 2 stitches over the stitches on the holder—30 (36) stitches.

upper hand

Knit rounds until the piece measures 2 (3)" (5 [7.5]cm) above the thumb gusset.

shape top

Round 1: *K4, k2tog; repeat from * around—25 (30) stitches.

Round 2: Knit.

Round 3: *K3, k2tog; repeat from * around—20 (24) stitches.

Round 4: Knit.

Round 5: *K2, k2tog; repeat from * around—15 (18) stitches.

Round 6: Knit.

Round 7: *K1, k2tog; repeat from * around—10 (12) stitches.

Round 8: Knit.

Round 9: *K2tog; repeat from * around—5 (6) stitches.

Cut the yarn, leaving a long end. Use the yarn needle to thread the end through the remaining stitches. Draw together tightly and fasten off.

thumb

Slip the thumb stitches from the holder back to 1 larger double-pointed needle. Join yarn and cast on 4 stitches—12 (14) stitches. Work back and forth on 2 double-pointed needles in stockinette stitch (knit on right side, purl on wrong side) until the thumb measures 1½ (2)" (3.5 [5]cm) from the last row of the thumb gusset, ending with a wrong-side row.

Next row: K2tog across—6 (7) stitches.

Cut the yarn, leaving a long end. Use the yarn needle to thread the end through the remaining stitches. Draw together tightly and fasten off.

FINISHING

Sew the thumb seam on the Medium and Large Mittens.

Using the yarn needle and B, duplicate stitch the Scottie Dog motif to the front of each Mitten. Follow the Scottie Dog chart and center the Scottie Dog motif on the front of the Mittens.

Using the red worsted-weight yarn, embroider a straight-stitch collar on each dog.

Weave in ends.

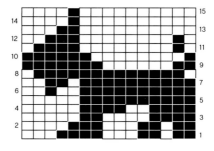

☐ #150 Silver (A)
■ #153 Black (B)

Glossary

KNITTING TERMS

Bind Off • Securing stitches on a completed knitted item to keep them from unraveling by lifting the first stitch over the second, the second over the third, etc.

Bind Off in Ribbing • Work in the rib pattern as you bind off by knitting the knit stitches and purling the purl stitches.

Cast On • Form a foundation row by making loops on the knitting needle.

Circular Needle • Needles joined by a flexible cord connecting the two ends. They allow you to work around and around to knit a tube and can also be used as regular needles to knit in rows.

Decrease • Reduce the number of stitches in a row; for example, knit two stitches together (k2tog).

Double-Pointed Needle • Straight, usually short needles with points on both ends.

Garter Stitch • Knit all stitches every row.

Gauge • Gauge is the number of stitches per row and per inch that you measure when you do a swatch. Gauge affects the size of your finished project. Make a gauge swatch before starting any project.

Grafting • Grafting joins knitting seamlessly by mimicking a row of stitches. It is also sometimes called Kitchener stitch.

To graft, thread a yarn needle with a length of yarn. Place the two pieces to be joined with the right sides facing and hold the knitting needles in your left hand.
*Pass the wool needle knitwise through the first stitch on the front needle and slip the stitch off the knitting needle. Pass the wool needle purlwise through the second stitch on the same needle, leaving the stitch on the needle. Pass purlwise through the first stitch on the back knitting needle and slip the stitch off, then pass knitwise through the second stitch on the same needle, leaving the stitch on the needle. Repeat from *.

Increase • Add to the number of stitches in a row—for example, by knitting in front and back of a stitch.

Intarsia • To create blocks of different colors, knit each color section with a different length of yarn.

Knit 2 Together • (k2tog) Knit two stitches together.

Knit 2 Together Back • (k2togb) Knit 2 stitches together through the back of the stitches.

Knitwise • Insert the needle into the stitch as if to knit.

Make One • With the tip of the needle, lift the strand between the last stitch knitted and the next stitch on the left-hand needle, place the strand on the left-hand needle, and knit into the back of it to increase one stitch.

Pick Up and Knit (Purl) • Knit (or purl) into the loops along an edge.

Place Marker • Loop a piece of contrasting yarn or a store-bought stitch marker onto the needle between stitches to mark a place in the pattern.

Purlwise • Insert the needle into the stitch as if to purl.

Ribbing • Columns of knitted and purled stitches. Ribbing does not roll like stockinette stitch and is stretchy, so it is often used on edges of knitted items.

Selvage Stitch • Edge stitch that helps to make seaming easier.

Ssk • Slip 2 stitches knitwise one at a time, then knit the slipped stitches together through the back of the stitches.

Stockinette Stitch • Knit on the right side; purl on the wrong side.

Stitch Holder • Holds "live" stitches that need to be worked later.

Stranding • Working with more than one color of yarn and carrying it across the back (wrong side) of the work. If the distance between color changes is not too great (fewer than five stitches) then the yarn that is not being used can be left at the back (wrong side) of the work until it is required; then it is simply knitted or purled in the usual way. This creates a series of loops or "floats" at the back (wrong side) of the work.

Three-Needle Bind-off • With the right side of two pieces facing and the needles parallel, insert a third needle into the first stitch on each needle and knit them together as if one stitch. Knit the next two stitches the same way. Pass the first stitch on the third needle over the second stitch and off the needle. Repeat until one stitch remains on the third needle. Cut yarn and pull tail through the last stitch.

Weave in Ends • Cut yarn to 3" (7.5cm) strand. With a tapestry needle, weave the yarn up and over stitches. Run the yarn either along the selvage edge or across the back (wrong side) of the work.

Work Even • Continue in the specified pattern without increasing or decreasing.

Yarn Bobbin • Used in multicolor/intarsia knitting. Each color of yarn is wound around a separate bobbin to prevent the yarn from tangling.

Yarn/Tapestry Needle • Used to seam garments and weave in loose ends.

Resources

Throughout this book, the yarns called for are listed by name and brand in the materials section of each pattern. Below is a list of all the yarns called for in the book. These suppliers carry gorgeous ranges of yarns and colors as well as the tools, accessories, and embellishments no knitter should be without. To locate a retailer in your area, call or visit the following websites.

CLASSIC WOOL

Paton's

888-368-8401

www.patonsyarns.com

FRISKY

JCA/Reynolds

978-597-8794

www.jcacrafts.com

LAMB'S PRIDE WORSTED WEIGHT

Brown Sheep Company, Inc.

800-826-9136

www.brownsheep.com

LION CASHMERE BLEND

Lion Brand Yarn Company

800-258-YARN

www.lionbrand.com

NATURAL ANGORA

Bloomingdale Farm Angoras

740-733-6283

www.hometown.aol.com/

robertsconsultan/index.html

ACCESSORIES (scissor fobs, stitch markers, etc.)

Zecca

413-528-0066

www.zecca.net

karen@zecca.net

ACCESSORIES (pom-poms, buttons, fabric or craft glue, felt fabric, wiggle, crystal, and frog eyes)

CreateForLess

866.333.4463

www.createforless.com

Yarn Substitution Guide

You can be a bit flexible about your yarn choice so long as the yarn you've chosen produces the specified gauge (more information on page 10). Feel free to experiment with different textured yarns and colors to produce entirely different results. All the projects featured in this book are made using a medium/worsted weight yarn, (4) medium, which generally yields 16–20 stitches on needles size US 7–9 (4.5mm–5.5mm).

CLASSIC WOOL BY PATON'S: (for Cheddar the Mouse only) Lion Wool by Lion Brand Yarn Co. and Ultra Alpaca by Berroco.

FRISKY BY REYNOLDS: Tiffany by Lion Brand Yarn Co.; Ballet by Trendsetter; Plush, Softy, or Zap, all by Berroco.

LAMB'S PRIDE WORSTED WEIGHT: Aurora 8 by Karabella Yarns; Bazic Wool by Classic Elite; 1824 by Mission Falls.

LION CASHMERE BLEND BY LION BRAND YARN CO.: Bazic Wool, Four Seasons, Lavish, Lush, or Charmed, by Classic Elite; 1824 by Mission Falls.

NATURAL ANGORA BY BLOOMINGDALE FARM ANGORAS: Jolie Angora by Tahki Stacy Charles; Anny Blatt Super Angora; and 100% Angora & Angora Blend (Cocoon) by Trendsetter.

Here are some general substitution suggestions that will work for any of the yarns called for in the book: Pure Merino and Peruvia, both by Berroco; Bazic Wool, Four Seasons; Lavish; La Gran Mohair, Lush, or Charmed, all by Classic Elite; 1824 by Mission Falls; Andean Alpaca and Lite Lopi, both by Reynolds; Orchid Yarns by Harrisville Designs; Alpaca Silk and Cashmerino Aran, both by Debbie Bliss; Cascade 220, Cascade 220 Tweed, Cascade 220 Solid, and Cascade 220 Superwash, all by Cascade Yarns; Worsted Hand Dyes by Blue Sky Alpaca; Aurora 8 by Karabella; and Manos del Uruguay Wool by Manos del Uruguay Yarn.

Acknowledgments

Special thanks to Jeff Wozniak and Stephanie Klose for their expert copyediting; Karen Hay for her technical editing expertise; Debra Hughes, Kelly Wilson, and Doris Pearce—the three best knitters in the world—for making samples; Karen Hennesey at Zecca for generously donating her precious works of art; Brown Sheep Yarn Company for their generous gift of great yarns.

My editor, Christina Schoen, for her insightful advice and guidance.

Potter Craft, Rosy Ngo, Chi Ling Moy, and Isa Loundon for your enthusiasm and all the special people at Random House for their vision, encouragement, and support.

Thank you Potter Craft/Random House for the opportunity to make this book a reality; it is truly a dream come true.

Index

NOTE: Numbers in bold (for example, **49**) indicate photographs.